Introducing

SHAKESPEARE

International Thomson Publishing, 1997

Published simultaneously in 1997 by International Thomson Limited:

ITP Nelson Canada | **South-Western Educational Publishing (U.S.A.)**
Nelson ITP (Australia) | **Thomas Nelson United Kingdom**

ISBN 0-17-606610-1

Cataloguing in Publication Data

Shakespeare, William, 1564-1616
Introducing Shakespeare

(The global Shakespeare series)
ISBN 0-17-606610-1

I. Saliani, Dom. II. Title. III. Series.

PR2768.S24 1996 822.3'3 C96-990040-6

Project Managers: Tara Steele (Canada)
Jackie Tidey (Australia)
Laurie Wendell (U.S.A.)
Series Designer: Liz Harasymczuk
Cover Artwork: Silvester Harding (1745-1809) from *Drawings for Shakespeare, Portraits based on paintings in noblemen's and gentlemen's homes.*
Composition Analyst: Daryn Dewalt
Production Coordinator: Donna Brown
Permissions: Vicki Gould
Research: Lisa Brant

Printed and bound in Canada

Visit us on our website:
http://www.thomson.com

3 4 5 6 ITIB 02 01 00

THE GLOBAL SHAKESPEARE SERIES

Introducing SHAKESPEARE

SERIES EDITORS

Dom Saliani   Chris Ferguson   Dr. Tim Scott

I(T)P *International Thomson Publishing*

Albany • Bonn • Boston • Cincinnati • Detroit • London • Madrid • Melbourne • Mexico City • New York • Pacific Grove • Paris • San Francisco • Singapore • Tokyo • Toronto • Washington

Contents

Prologue

Act One: Speak the speech ... trippingly

Act Two: The play's the thing ...

Act Three: Not marble, nor the gilded monuments shall outlive these Sonnets

Epilogue

Prologue

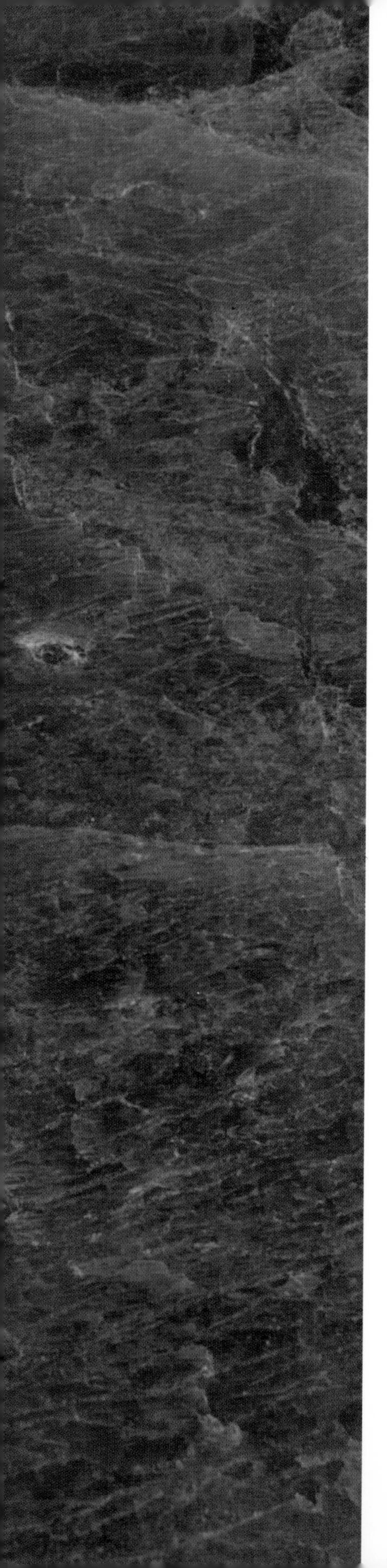

O for a muse of fire

O for a muse of fire, that would ascend
The brightest heaven of invention,
A kingdom for a stage, princes to act,
And monarchs to behold the swelling scene!
(Henry V, Prologue)

Welcome to the world of William Shakespeare. If this is your first exposure to Shakespeare, then you are about to embark on an exciting adventure!

If it's the pageantry of history that you like, you're in luck. Shakespeare's plays delve into the most exciting aspects of British and Roman history. If fantasy is what you crave, then come aboard and together we will set sail for magical islands and mythical times. We will venture into forests filled with fairies and sprites. If it's great tragedies that inspire you, be prepared to be moved by unforgettable characters such as Romeo and Juliet, Macbeth and Lady Macbeth, Hamlet, and Cleopatra. If it's laughter you prefer, prepare to meet the greatest comic writer of all time — William Shakespeare!

Shakespeare's works, whether they be tragedy or comedy, fantasy or history, deal with characters who are larger than life and yet very real. So real in fact, that one cannot help but identify with their fortunes and failures, characteristics and conflicts.

There is fire and life in Shakespeare which still burn brightly even after four hundred years. Come closer and you too will feel the passion and the power of his words.

Who was William Shakespeare?

In 1623, Ben Jonson heralded Shakespeare as being "Not of an age but for all time." Several hundred years later, Russian novelist Leo Tolstoy (1828–1910) declared that "Shakespeare is crude, immoral, vulgar, and senseless." Who was right? Perhaps, like most things in life, it depends on your point of view and attitude. Shakespeare himself wrote that "Nothing is either good or bad but thinking makes it so."

Not much is known about Shakespeare's life. As a matter of fact, there are many who believe that we do not even know who the author of the plays really was. Some think he was the son of a glove-maker and was born in Stratford-Upon-Avon in 1564 and died there in 1616.

Still others believe that the plays contain too much detailed knowledge of life in the court to have been written by a commoner, and they offer noblemen such as Sir Francis Bacon and Edward De Vere, 17th Earl of Oxford, as their candidates for the authorship. Some even suggest that Queen Elizabeth or King James I wrote the plays.

We may never fully resolve the identity of William Shakespeare but one thing that most can certainly agree with is that he was the greatest writer ever produced by Western civilization.

But Shakespeare also has his critics as the following quotations will reveal:

> "Shakespeare is a drunken savage with some imagination whose plays can please only in London and Canada."
>
> – Voltaire (1694 – 1778)

> "Shakespeare should not be put into the hands of the young without the warning that the foolish things in his plays were written to please the foolish, the filthy for the filthy, and the brutal for the brutal; and that if out of veneration for his genius we were led to admire or even tolerate such things, we may be thereby not conforming ourselves to him, but only degrading ourselves to the level of his audience ..."
>
> – Robert Bridges

> "I have tried lately to read Shakespeare, and found it so intolerably dull that it nauseated me."
>
> – Charles Darwin (1809 – 1882)

Not everyone despises Shakespeare as much as the preceding quotations would indicate. Here are some opinions expressed by those who admire Shakespeare:

> "A royal trait that belongs to Shakespeare is his cheerfulness. He delights in the world, in man, in woman, for the lovely light that sparkles from them. Beauty, the spirit of joy and hilarity, he sheds over the Universe. If he should appear in any company of human souls, who would not march in his troop?"
>
> – Ralph Waldo Emerson (1803 – 1882)

> As I declare our Poet, him
> Whose insight makes all others dim.
> A thousand poets pried at life,
> But only one amid the strife
> Rose to be Shakespeare.
>
> – Robert Browning (1812 – 1889)

> "He was the man who of all modern, and perhaps ancient poets had the largest and most comprehensive soul. All the images of Nature were still present to him, and he drew them not laboriously but luckily: when he describes any thing, you more than see it, you feel it too."
>
> – John Dryden (1631 – 1700)

> "The remarkable thing about Shakespeare is that he is really very good — in spite of all the people who say he is very good."
>
> – Robert Graves (1895 – 1985)

> "Like a miraculous celestial Light-ship, woven all of sheet-lighting and sunbeams."
>
> – Thomas Carlyle (1795 – 1881)

"In Shakespeare the birds sing, the rushes are clothed with green, hearts love, souls suffer, the clouds wanders, it is hot, it is cold, night falls, time passes, forests and multitudes speak, the vast eternal dream hovers over all. Sap and blood, all forms of the multiple reality, actions and ideas, man and humanity, the living and the life, solitudes, cities, religions, diamonds and pearls, dunghills and charnel houses, the ebb and flow of beings, the steps of comers and goers, all, all are in Shakespeare. . ."

– Victor Hugo (1802 – 1885)

"Shakespeare is a good raft whereon to float securely down the stream of time; fasten yourself to that and your immortality is safe."

– George Henry Lewes (1817 – 1878)

- How do you feel about Shakespeare or about the prospects of studying his works? Explore your initial thoughts and position concerning Shakespeare by writing several paragraphs.

- Conduct an opinion poll. Ask a variety of people (teachers, parents, friends, bus drivers, police officers, dentists, etc.) what they think of Shakespeare and record their opinions. Come up with at least three questions to ask these people. Tally the results and form some conclusions. After you have done so, re-evaluate your initial impressions of the Bard.

FRANK & ERNEST® by Bob Thaves

Frank & Ernest reprinted by permission of Newspaper Enterprise Association, Inc.

What did Shakespeare write?

Shakespeare wrote at least 37 plays. Of these, only 18 were printed in his lifetime.

The plays first appeared in quarto form. To create a quarto, large sheets of paper were folded into four and then bound. The result was a book slightly larger than today's paperbacks. In 1623, the complete works of Shakespeare were printed in what is known as the First Folio. A folio is a much larger book, which is made by folding large sheets of paper in two and then binding them.

Shakespeare's plays can be organized according to four broad categories. They are:

Comedies

A full third of Shakespeare's plays were comedies. He was considered the best writer of his day for this particular genre. Today we think of comedies as works that make us laugh. According to the classical definition of the term, a comedy is a work that ends happily. Many of Shakespeare's comedies actually deal with serious themes. However, they do have many bright comical moments, hilarious characters, and witty dialogue. The happy endings in these plays, more often than not, involve marriage or the reconciliation of lovers.

The Comedies:

A Midsummer Night's Dream
The Comedy of Errors
Love's Labour's Lost
The Taming of the Shrew
The Two Gentlemen of Verona
The Merchant of Venice
Much Ado About Nothing
As You Like It
Twelfth Night
All's Well That Ends Well
Measure for Measure
The Merry Wives of Windsor

Tragedies

Shakespeare's tragedies are among the most highly respected works of literature ever created. In these plays, tragic heroes grapple with important issues like love, death, revenge, jealousy, ambition, and ingratitude, to name a few. By definition, a tragedy is a work that ends unhappily. The protagonist suffers a tragic end as a result of some inner flaw or error in judgement. Some of the greatest speeches ever written appear in Shakespeare's tragedies.

The Tragedies:

Troilus and Cressida
Timon of Athens
Coriolanus
Julius Caesar
Antony and Cleopatra
Titus Andronicus
King Lear
Hamlet
Macbeth
Romeo and Juliet
Othello

Histories
Ten of Shakespeare's plays deal with English history. The period covered in these plays extends from the time of King John, who reigned 1199 to 1216, to the time of King Henry VIII, who died in 1547. These plays basically served to arouse patriotism and loyalty to crown and country. The plays also warned about the dangers of civil war. Despite the fact that these plays are considered histories, Shakespeare does not hesitate to alter facts to tell a better story.

The Histories:
King John
Richard II
Henry IV, Part One
Henry IV, Part Two
Henry V
Henry VI, Part One
Henry VI, Part Two
Henry VI, Part Three
Richard III
Henry VIII

Romances
Among the more interesting of Shakespeare's inventions are his Romances, which may also be considered "tragi-comedies" in that they begin in a tragic mode but end happily. These plays often involve sea travel, wrecks and adventure, families being separated and reunited in the end, and tragic misunderstandings followed by forgiveness and reconciliation.

The Romances:
Pericles
Cymbeline
The Winter's Tale
The Tempest

As well as writing plays, Shakespeare gained credibility and critical acceptance by writing poetry. He wrote two long narrative poems, a series of sonnets, a collection of short verse, and an extremely short, enigmatic piece called "The Phoenix and the Turtle." Critics are still puzzled as to what this work is all about.

The Poems:
Venus and Adonis
The Rape of Lucrece
The Sonnets
The Passionate Pilgrim
The Phoenix and the Turtle

- Choose one of the plays that you are interested in knowing more about. Without reading the play, compile some basic information on it. What is it about? Who are the major characters? Where does the action take place and during which time period? Write a short plot summary of the play to present to the class.
- Many of Shakespeare's plays have been turned into feature films. Visit your local video store and compile a list of the movies you find there that are based on Shakespeare's work. In groups, choose a title to rent. Pick a convenient time, make some popcorn, and spend an evening with the Bard. Report to the class how the video compares with what you expected a Shakespeare play to be like.

Words, words, words

POLONIUS: What do you read, my lord?
HAMLET: Words, words, words.

(Hamlet – Act 2, Scene 2)

According to the *Harvard Concordance*, Shakespeare wrote a total of 884,647 words. Furthermore, his vocabulary was enormous, even by today's standards. He used, by some counts, close to 29,000 different words.

What is even more remarkable is that Shakespeare is credited with being the first user of close to 9,000 different words. This does not mean that he invented these words. It just means that he is recognized as being the first person to use the words in print.

Many of these words were created by anglicizing Latin words by adding suffixes. It should be remembered that during Shakespeare's time, Latin was the official language of law, religion, medicine, commerce and to a great part, literature. English was considered a primitive language, and too unsophisticated to express powerful and sensitive sentiments and ideas. Shakespeare changed all this.

Here is a brief sampling of words Shakespeare is credited with introducing into the English language. To find more, just flip through your library's *Oxford English Dictionary* and browse.

accommodation
admirable
amazement
arch-villain
assassination
batty
bloodsucking
bold-faced
cater
cheap
circumstantial
cold-blooded
coldhearted
countless
critical
domineering
dwindle
employment
equivocal
eventful
exposure
fairyland
fashionable
flowery
fortune-teller
freezing
generous
go-between
grime
impartial
inaudible
inauspicious
invulnerable
lapse
laughable
lonely
madcap
majestic
monumental
motionless
newsmonger
overpower

pale-faced
paternal
perusal
pious
priceless
radiance
reliance
shooting star
slugabed
stillborn
successful
tardiness
unearthly
unpolluted
unquestioned
unreal
vulnerable
watchdog
zany

- Go to your local library and consult the *Oxford English Dictionary.* Find first-usage references for at least 10 of the above words. You will need to provide the meaning of the word as well as the quotation from the Shakespearean work in which the word first appeared.
- Scan the *Oxford English Dictionary* to find at least five more words that were first used by Shakespeare.
- Create a crossword puzzle. If you have access to a CD-ROM or the Internet, you can utilize the search functions to locate Shakespearean quotations that contain words from the above list to use as your clues.
- Use at least 10 of the above words in sentences. You may choose to combine this activity with words from the "Shakespearean Insults" list on page 19 to create Shakespearean sounding sentences.
- For at least 10 of the above words, search the dictionary for other words that are related to or derived from them. List as many as you can find.

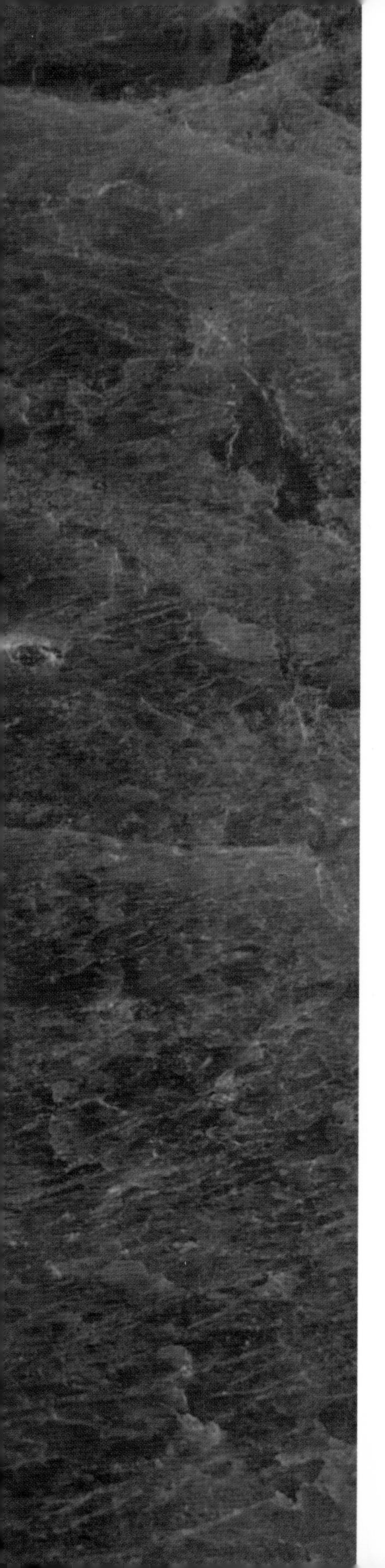

Quoting Shakespeare — everybody does it!

"Shake was a dramatist of note;
He lived by writing things to quote."

– *H.C. Brunner*

One student criticized the play *Hamlet* because, in his opinion, it was made up of a whole string of clichés. This may seem true to us today, but when Shakespeare first wrote the play, his words were fresh and new. What is certainly indisputable is that Shakespeare is very much a part of our everyday language.

The next time you watch a Sherlock Holmes movie and you hear the famous sleuth say that "The game is afoot," you should know that he is quoting Shakespeare.

Here are some other common phrases and lines that were first spoken by Shakespeare's characters. How many have you recently heard or used?

an eyesore
apple of her eye
as white as the driven snow
bated breath
breathe one's last
budge an inch
dead as a doornail
devil incarnate
dog will have his day
eaten me out of house and home
for goodness' sake
foregone conclusion
fortune's fool
green-eyed monster
household words
in my heart of hearts
into thin air
it smells to heaven
Knock, knock! Who's there?
laughing stock
man of steel
murder most foul
neither rhyme nor reason
not a mouse stirring
O, brave new world

one fell swoop
pomp and circumstance
primrose path
remembrance of things past
short shrift
sound and fury
strange bedfellows
sweets to the sweet
the be-all and the end-all
the play's the thing
the game is up
the very witching time of night
to be, or not to be
to thine own self be true
tower of strength
too much of a good thing
we have seen better days
what the dickens
what's done is done

- **Be a bard or storyteller:** Write a short story or poem in which you use as many of the above familiar phrases as you can.

- We quote Shakespeare every day and his words have become a part of our language. For the next few weeks, scan newspapers, magazines, and song lyrics, listen to TV and movie dialogue, and pay attention to everyday conversations. Be on the look-out for examples of Shakespeare's words and phrases being used. If the quotation appears in a print medium, cut out and paste or copy the page upon which it appears. If the quotation is used in any other medium, make a note of how it was used. Share your findings with the class in the form of a report with conclusions.

Shakespearean insults

There is nothing more impressive than a Shakespearean sounding insult. Read the following insults from several of Shakespeare's most popular plays. You may wish to memorize some of them to use when an appropriate occasion should arise.

As You Like It:

- His brain is as dry as the remainder biscuit after a long voyage.
- Let's meet as little as we can.
- I do desire we may be better strangers.

Hamlet:

- Bloody, bawdy, villain!
  Remorseless, treacherous, lecherous, kindless villain!
- I took thee for thy better.
- You are a fishmonger.

Henry V:

- [Thou] vain, giddy, shallow, humorous youth!
- What an arrant, rascally, beggarly, lousy knave it is.
- [Thy] face is not worth sunburning.

Julius Caesar:

- You blocks, you stones, you worse than senseless things!
- I spurn thee like a cur out of my way.

Macbeth:

- How now, you secret, black, and midnight hags!
- Thou lily-livered boy!
- Thou bloodier villain than terms can give thee out!

A Midsummer Night's Dream:

- You juggler! You canker–blossom!
- Get you gone, you dwarf; you minimus ... You bead, you acorn!

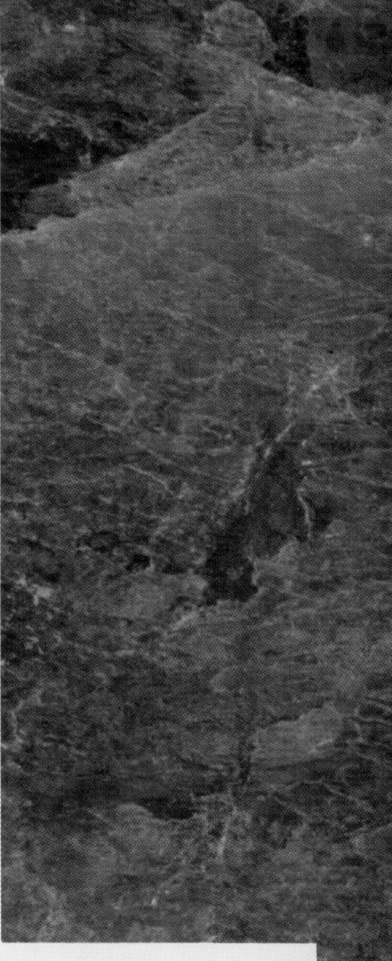

Much Ado About Nothing:

- [Thou] art duller than a great thaw.
- Neighbours, you are tedious.
- You have such a February face,
  So full of frost, of storm, and cloudiness.

Romeo and Juliet:

- [He] loves to hear himself talk, and will speak more in a minute than he will stand to in a month.
- The love I bear thee can afford no better term than this: thou art a villain.
- [Thou art] a braggart, a rogue, a villain, that fights by the book of arithmetic.

Taming of the Shrew:

- There's small choice in rotten apples.
- You heedless joltheads and unmannered slaves!
- I know she is an irksome brawling scold.

Reprinted with special permission of North America Syndicate.

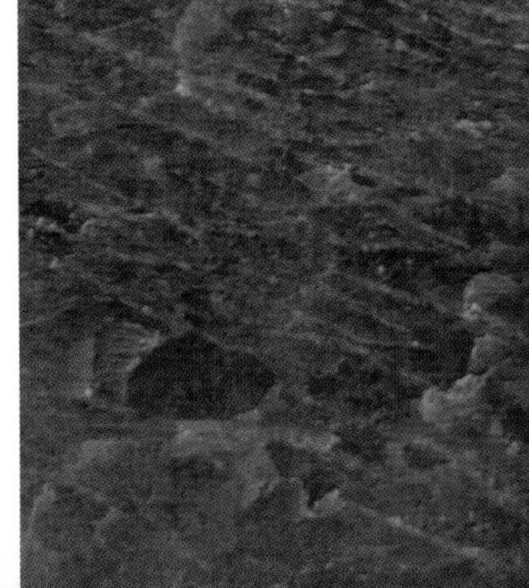

Create your own Shakespearean sounding insults

The words in the following lists all come from Shakespeare's plays. To create your own Shakespearean sounding insults, choose a word from each of the columns and begin your invective with "Thou" or "You."

Column A	Column B	Column C
abhorred	accursed	acquaintance
bloody	abominable	canker-blossom
brawling	base	block
complete	brutish	clown
craven	calumnious	corruptor
currish	crafty	counterfeit
detestable	disloyal	coward
dishonest	dizzy-eyed	defiler
droning	doting	dwarf
dull	execrable	fiend
errant	fantastical	filth
false	gross	fishmonger
fawning	headstrong	fool
flattering	hollow-hearted	fustilarian
foolish	horrible	gossip
foul	hyperbolical	hellhound
gleeking	ill-breeding	hugger-mugger
goatish	impudent	jolthead
idle-pated	insolent	knave
impertinent	irksome	lewdster
infectious	jealous	louse
loathsome	joyless	lout
loggerheaded	leprous	lunatic
malignant	lily–livered	minimus
mewling	loathsomest	minion
mindless	lowborn	miscreant
naughty	madcap	monster
pestilent	mangy	moon-calf
petty	motley-minded	paraquito
puking	mumbling	peasant
puny	noise–maker	peacock
rank	notorious	quintessence
saucy	onion-eyed	rascal
scurvy	peevish	ratcatcher
shallow	plume-plucked	rioter
strange	pox-marked	rogue
surly	proud-minded	ruffian
tedious	putrified	sluggard
unseemly	rotten	swine
vain	rude	thing
villainous	rump-fed	traitor
waspish	scornful	varlot
wayward	unjust	vassal
worthless	untaught	villain
wretched	vile	worm

Speeches

Act One:

"Speak the speech ... trippingly" (Hamlet)

Hamlet, Macbeth, Romeo, Juliet, Cleopatra, Portia, Julius Caesar, Beatrice, and the list goes on. Shakespeare's protagonists are among the most memorable characters in literature. They are unforgettable firstly because of their humanity — they are realistically portrayed and easy to identify with. Perhaps another reason they are so memorable is because of their great speeches.

In this chapter, you will be introduced to these characters and their greatest speeches. Remember at all times that these speeches are set in a dramatic context and each has an important function to perform in the play it comes from.

You may be asked to present one or more of the speeches. If you are, remember to heed the advice Hamlet gave the actors:

> "Speak the speech ... trippingly on the tongue .... Do not saw the air too much with your hand, ... but use all gently .... Be not too tame neither .... Suit the action to the word, the word to the action, with this special observation, that you overstep not the modesty of nature."

Hamlet goes on to discuss the purpose of drama and what he said four hundred years ago still applies today. It is "to hold, as it were, the mirror up to nature." The actor's duty, therefore, is to create an illusion or reflection of reality. This can be quite a challenge but with a little planning, preparation, and practice, you can do it.

All the world's a stage

(As You Like It – Act 2, Scene 7)

Jaques is a melancholy cynic who has exiled himself to the Forest of Arden. Here he offers his unique and memorable metaphor for life.

JAQUES:

All the world's a stage,
And all the men and women merely players.
They have their exits and their entrances
And one man in his time plays many parts,
His acts being seven ages. At first the infant, 5
Mewling and puking in the nurse's arms.
And then the whining school-boy, with his satchel
And shining morning face, creeping like snail
Unwillingly to school. And then the lover,
Sighing like furnace, with a woeful ballad 10
Made to his mistress' eyebrow. Then a soldier,
Full of strange oaths and bearded like the pard,
Jealous in honour, sudden and quick in quarrel,
Seeking the bubble reputation
Even in the cannon's mouth. And then the justice, 15
In fair round belly with good capon lined,
With eyes severe and beard of formal cut,
Full of wise saws and modern instances.
And so he plays his part. The sixth age shifts
Into the lean and slippered pantaloon, 20
With spectacles on nose and pouch on side,
His youthful hose, well saved, a world too wide
For his shrunk shank. And his big manly voice,
Turning again toward childish treble, pipes
And whistles in his sound. Last scene of all, 25
That ends this strange eventful history,
Is second childishness and mere oblivion,
Sans teeth, sans eyes, sans taste, sans everything.

In 1599, the Globe Theatre opened for business. The motto of the theatre was: *Totus Mundi agit histrionem* – which translates as *All the world's a stage.*

6. *mewling* – crying
12. *pard* – leopard
18. *saws* – sayings
20. *pantaloon* – foolish old man

pantaloon

27. *oblivion* – forgetfulness
28. *sans* – French for "without"

The cynical Jaques may appear philosophical on the surface, but notice that each of his vignettes is inherently comic. The effect of his speech is amusement rather than reflection on the human condition.

To thine own self be true

(Hamlet – Act 1, Scene 3)

Laertes is about to leave Denmark to resume his studies in Paris. But before he goes, his father, Polonius, has some words of advice for him.

POLONIUS:

Give thy thoughts no tongue,
Nor any unproportioned thought his act.
Be thou familiar, but by no means vulgar.
Those friends thou hast, and their adoption tried,
Grapple them to thy soul with hoops of steel, 5
But do not dull thy palm with entertainment
Of each new-hatched, unfledged comrade. Beware
Of entrance to a quarrel, but being in,
Bear it that the opposed may beware of thee.
Give every man thy ear, but few thy voice. 10
Take each man's censure, but reserve thy judgment.
Costly thy habit as thy purse can buy,
But not expressed in fancy — rich, not gaudy,
For the apparel oft proclaims the man...
Neither a borrower nor a lender be, 15
For loan oft loses both itself and friend,
And borrowing dulls the edge of husbandry.
This above all: to thine own self be true,
And it must follow, as the night the day
Thou canst not then be false to any man. 20

2. *unproportioned* – unruly
3. "Be sociable but don't lower yourself by being too friendly with anyone."
4. *adoption tried* – friendship tested
6. *dull thy palm* – shake hands with, make friends
9. *Bear it* – conduct yourself in such a way
11. *censure* – opinion
12. *habit* – clothing
17. *husbandry* – skill in money management

18. *to thine own self be true* – Noble words and great advice! In the play, however, Polonius is a foolish, self-serving individual. Therefore, we need to look at his words more carefully. A less noble interpretation of this line in particular may yield something like: *Look out for your own interests first.*

"Are you out of your mind?"

The quality of mercy

(The Merchant of Venice – Act 4, Scene 1)

Antonio, a merchant of Venice, has borrowed 3000 ducats from a money-lender named Shylock. Antonio agreed that if he could not repay the loan in three months, he would forfeit a pound of his flesh. The allotted time has passed and Shylock is in court, demanding justice and his pound of flesh. Young Portia, disguised as a lawyer, pleads with Shylock for mercy.

This speech contains some of the best known and most often quoted lines in all of Shakespeare's works. Here Shakespeare, through Portia, builds an eloquent case for the value of mercy over justice.

PORTIA:

The quality of mercy is not strained,
It droppeth as the gentle rain from heaven
Upon the place beneath. It is twice blest –
It blesseth him that gives and him that takes.
'Tis mightiest in the mightiest. It becomes 5
The throned monarch better than his crown.
His sceptre shows the force of temporal power,
The attribute to awe and majesty,
Wherein doth sit the dread and fear of kings.
But mercy is above this sceptred sway. 10
It is enthroned in the hearts of kings,
It is an attribute to God himself,
And earthly power doth then show likest God's
When mercy seasons justice.

7. *sceptre* – a staff held by a ruler as a symbol of authority
temporal – earthly; bound by time

14. *seasons* – tempers, moderates

The lunatic, the lover and the poet

(A Midsummer Night's Dream – Act 5, Scene 1)

Duke Theseus has just heard a fantastic story about what has occurred in the forest the night before. Because the story was told by four young lovers, he dismisses it as being a wild figment of their imagination. And these are his reasons:

THESEUS:

Lovers and madmen have such seething brains,
Such shaping fantasies, that apprehend
More than cool reason ever comprehends.
The lunatic, the lover and the poet
Are of imagination all compact. 5
One sees more devils than vast hell can hold,
That is, the madman. The lover, all as frantic,
Sees Helen's beauty in a brow of Egypt.
The poet's eye, in fine frenzy rolling,
Doth glance from heaven to earth, from earth to heaven 10
And as imagination bodies forth
The forms of things unknown. The poet's pen
Turns them to shapes and gives to airy nothing
A local habitation and a name.
Such tricks hath strong imagination, 15
That if it would but apprehend some joy,
It comprehends some bringer of that joy,
Or in the night, imagining some fear,
How easy is a bush supposed a bear!

1. *seething* – over-active
2. *shaping fantasies* – creative imaginations
apprehend – imagine
5. *compact* – of the same form
8. *Helen* – Helen of Troy was considered the most beautiful woman in the ancient Greek world
brow of Egypt: i.e. gypsy

9. *fine frenzy*: Poets were considered to be divinely inspired and as such, not in their natural wits.

11. *bodies forth* – translates into familiar forms

There is a willow

(Hamlet – Act 4, Scene 7)

The Queen has the unhappy task of informing Laertes that his sister, Ophelia, has just drowned. Just previous to her death, Ophelia had lost her mind due to grief over the murder of her father and the departure of her love, Hamlet.

QUEEN:

There is a willow grows askant the brook
That shows his hoary leaves in the glassy stream.
Therewith fantastic garlands did she make
Of crow-flowers, nettles, daisies, and long purples
That liberal shepherds give a grosser name, 5
But our cold maids do dead men's fingers call them.
There, on the pendent boughs her coronet weeds
Clambering to hang, an envious sliver broke,
When down her weedy trophies and herself
Fell in the weeping brook. Her clothes spread wide, 10
And, mermaid-like, awhile they bore her up,
Which time she chanted snatches of old tunes,
As one incapable of her own distress,
Or like a creature native and indued
Unto that element. But long it could not be 15
Till that her garments, heavy with their drink,
Pulled the poor wretch from her melodious lay
To muddy death.

1. *askant* – slanting out over
2. *hoary* – greyish

6. *cold* – chaste
7. *coronet* – in the shape of a crown
8. *envious* – malicious

13. *incapable* – unable to comprehend
14. *native and indued* – born to and adapted

17. *lay* – song

In relating the description of Ophelia's death, Gertrude displays a knowledge that could only come from an eye-witness. If such is the case, one cannot help but ask, "Why didn't the eye-witness stop or help Ophelia?" Perhaps we need to grant Shakespeare his poetic licence and not ask too many questions.

Ophelia

Poor Ophelia sighed: "I deplore
The fact that young Hamlet's a bore.
He just talks to himself;
I'll be left on his shelf,
Or go mad by the end of Act IV."

Frank Richards

Out, damned spot!

(Macbeth – Act 5, Scene 1)

In their attempt to attain security and peace of mind, Macbeth and Lady Macbeth kill or have killed anyone who stands in their way. This tactic does not work and Lady Macbeth goes insane. During her sleepwalking episodes, she discloses dark secrets of their bloody deeds, as she tries to wash blood from her hands.

LADY MACBETH:

Yet here's a spot … Out, damned spot!
Out, I say! One - two - why then 'tis time to do it.
Hell is murky. Fie, my lord, fie! A soldier, and afeard?
What need we fear who knows it, when none can call our
power to account? Yet who would have thought the old 5
man to have had so much blood in him? …
The Thane of Fife had a wife. Where is she now?
What, will these hands never be clean?
No more of that, my lord, no more of that.
You mar all with this starting … 10
Here's the smell of the blood still. All the perfumes
of Arabia will not sweeten this little hand.
Oh, oh, oh! …
Wash your hands, put on your nightgown,
look not so pale. I tell you yet again, Banquo's buried. 15
He cannot come out on his grave.
To bed, to bed. There's knocking at the gate.
Come, come, come, come, give me your hand.
What's done cannot be undone. To bed, to bed, to bed.

3. *fie* – exclamation, expressing disgust

5. *the old man* – a reference to King Duncan, the first of the Macbeths' victims

7. Macduff, the Thane of Fife, left Scotland for England to rally forces against Macbeth. During his absence, Macduff's entire household is murdered by Macbeth's men.

8. A truly ironic line. After the killing of Duncan, Macbeth expresses the belief that his bloody hands will never come clean. Lady Macbeth counters with "A little water clears us of this deed."

15. *Banquo* – a reference to another of Macbeth's victims. After his murder, Banquo's ghost appears and sits at Macbeth's place at the banquet table.

17. *knocking* – Immediately following the killing of Duncan, a loud persistent knocking announces the arrival of Macduff.

Reprinted with special permission of North America Syndicate.

Forgeries of jealousy

(A Midsummer Night's Dream –
Act 2, Scene 1)

Titania and Oberon, Queen and King of the Fairies, have been arguing. They have gone so far as to accuse each other of being unfaithful. Here Titania recounts the disastrous effect their disagreement has had on the natural world.

TITANIA:

These are the forgeries of jealousy
And never since the middle summer's spring,
Met we on hill, in dale, forest, or mead,
By paved fountain or by rushy brook,
Or in the beached margent of the sea, 5
To dance our ringlets to the whistling wind,
But with thy brawls thou hast disturbed our sport.
Therefore the winds, piping to us in vain,
As in revenge, have sucked up from the sea
Contagious fogs, which falling in the land, 10
Hath every pelting river made so proud
That they have overborne their continents.
The ox hath therefore stretched his yoke in vain,
The ploughman lost his sweat, and the green corn
Hath rotted ere his youth attained a beard. 15
The fold stands empty in the drowned field,
And crows are fatted with the murrion flock; ...
The human mortals want their winter here;
No night is now with hymn or carol blest.
Therefore the moon, the governess of floods, 20
Pale in her anger, washes all the air,
That rheumatic diseases do abound.
And thorough this distemperature, we see
The seasons alter. Hoary headed frosts
Fall in the fresh lap of the crimson rose, 25
And on old Hiems' thin and and icy crown
An odorous chaplet of sweet summer buds
Is, as in mockery, set. The spring, the summer,
The childing autumn, angry winter, change
Their wonted liveries, and the mazed world, 30
By their increase, now knows not which is which.
And this same progeny of evils comes
From our debate, from our dissension.
We are their parents and original.

2. *middle summer's spring* – beginning of midsummer
4. *rushy* – edged with rushes
5. *beached margent* – beach
6. *ringlets* – circular dances
10. *contagious* – noxious
11. *pelting* – paltry
12. *overborne their continents* – caused flooding by overflowing their banks
14. *lost his sweat* – worked in vain
15. *ere* – before
17. *murrion* – diseased
18. *want* – lack
22. *That* – So that
26. *Hiems* – god of winter
29. *childing* – fruitful
30. *wonted liveries* – customary appearance
30. *mazed* – confused; amazed
31. *By their increase* – what they bring forth
32. *progeny* – off-spring

How tartly that gentleman looks

(Much Ado About Nothing – Act 2, Scene 1)

Young Beatrice is attracted to Benedict but will not admit it. Here she attempts to convince her family that she is not and never will be the marrying kind.

BEATRICE:

How tartly that gentleman looks. I never can see him but I am heart-burned an hour after... Lord, I could not endure a husband with a beard on his face, I had rather lie in the woolen ... What should I do with [a husband with no beard]? Dress him in my apparel and make him my waiting gentle-woman? He that hath a beard is more than a youth, and he that hath no beard is less than a man; and he that is more than a youth is not for me, and he that is less than a man, I am not for him. Therefore I will even take sixpence in earnest of the bear-ward, and lead his apes to hell ... but to the gate, and there will the devil meet me ... and say, "Get you to heaven, Beatrice, get you to heaven, here's no place for you maids." So deliver I up my apes, and away to Saint Peter. For the heavens, he shows me where the bachelors sit, and there live we as merry as the day is long.

1. *tartly* – sour

4. *lie in the woolen* – between scratchy woolen linen

10 – 11. *in earnest of the bear-ward* – payment in advance from the bear-keeper. During the Elizabethan period, bear-baiting was a popular form of entertainment. Audiences wagered on the outcome of competitions to the death between a bear chained to a stake and dogs.

Bear-baiting

11. *lead his apes to hell* – proverbial fate of women who died single

15. *bachelors* – unmarried males or females

To be, or not to be

(Hamlet – Act 3, Scene 1)

In what is possibly the most famous speech in dramatic history, Hamlet ponders the meaning of life and his fears of the after-life if he commits suicide.

HAMLET:

To be, or not to be, that is the question.
Whether 'tis nobler in the mind to suffer
The slings and arrows of outrageous fortune,
Or to take arms against a sea of troubles,
And by opposing end them. To die, to sleep, 5
No more; and by a sleep to say we end
The heart-ache and the thousand natural shocks
That flesh is heir to. 'Tis a consummation
Devoutly to be wished. To die, to sleep;
To sleep, perchance to dream — aye, there's the rub, 10
For in that sleep of death what dreams may come,
When we have shuffled off this mortal coil,
Must give us pause — there's the respect
That makes calamity of so long life.
For who would bear the whips and scorns of time, 15
The oppressor's wrong, the proud man's contumely,
The pangs of despised love, the law's delay,
The insolence of office and the spurns
That patient merit of the unworthy takes,
When he himself might his quietus make 20
With a bare bodkin? Who would fardels bear,
To grunt and sweat under a weary life,
But that the dread of something after death,
The undiscovered country from whose bourn
No traveller returns, puzzles the will 25
And makes us rather bear those ills we have
Than fly to others that we know not of?
Thus conscience does make cowards of us all,
And thus the native hue of resolution
Is sicklied over with the pale cast of thought, 30
And enterprises of great pith and moment
With this regard their currents turn awry,
And lose the name of action.

8. *consummation* – final ending

10. *rub* – obstacle

12. *shuffled* – discarded ... *coil* – life; body

16. *contumely* – humiliations
17. *law's delay* – the slowness of the process of law
18. *office* – officials
18 – 9. *spurns ... takes* – insults inflicted on worthy persons by inferiors with power
20. *quietus* – settle accounts
21. *fardels* – burden
bodkin – dagger

bodkin

24. *bourn* – borders
28. *conscience* – thinking
29. *native* – natural
32. *regard* – consideration
awry – veer in the wrong direction

Calvin and Hobbes
by WATTERSON ©1994
dist. by universal press syndicate 3-6
BLECCHHH
"TO BE ??
..OR.. NOT TO BE ?
* SIGHHH * THAT
IS THE
QUESTION.
WHETHER 'TIS NOBLER IN THE MIND TO SUFFER THE SLINGS AND ARROWS OF OUTRAGEOUS FORTUNE...
...OR TO TAKE ARMS AGAINST A SEA OF TROUBLES ... AND BY OPPOSING, END THEM?
THWUP
TO DIE: TO SLEEP; .. NO MORE!
AND BY A SLEEP TO SAY WE END THE HEARTACHE AND THE THOUSAND NATURAL SHOCKS THAT FLESH IS HEIR TO...
* SNIFF * 'TIS A CONSUMMATION DEVOUTLY TO BE WISHED!
TO DIE, TO SLEEP!
TO SLEEP, PERCHANCE TO DREAM: AY, THERE'S THE RUB!
.. FOR IN THAT SLEEP OF DEATH, WHAT DREAMS MAY COME WHEN WE HAVE SHUFFLED OFF THIS MORTAL COIL MUST GIVE US PAUSE."
Blink
Blink
FEEHEELINGGS
WO WO WO
YOU FINISHED THAT RIGHT UP! DID YOU LIKE IT?
LET'S NOT HAVE THIS EVER AGAIN.

Tomorrow, and tomorrow, and tomorrow

(Macbeth – Act 5, Scene 5)

The tyrant Macbeth is completely surrounded by his enemies. To make matters worse, he receives news that his wife has just killed herself. At this point, he sees no sense or purpose in life.

MACBETH:

Tomorrow, and tomorrow, and tomorrow
Creeps in this petty pace from day to day
To the last syllable of recorded time,
And all our yesterdays have lighted fools
The way to dusty death. Out, out, brief candle! 5
Life's but a walking shadow, a poor player,
That struts and frets his hour upon the stage
And then is heard no more. It is a tale
Told by an idiot, full of sound and fury,
Signifying nothing. 10

5. *dusty death* – Perhaps a reference to Genesis 3.19 – "For dust thou art and unto dust thou shalt return."
brief candle – short life

6. shadow – actors were frequently referred to as "shadows."

"Life is not a 'brief candle.' It is a splendid torch that I want to make burn as brightly as possible before handing it on to future generations."
– George Bernard Shaw (1856 – 1950), English playwright and essayist

Limerick

There once was a king named Macbeth;
A better king never drew breath;
The faults of his life
Were all due to his wife
The notorious Lady Macbeth

– Anonymous

I have immortal longings in me

(Antony and Cleopatra – Act 5, Scene 2)

Antony, Cleopatra's husband, has just died from a self-inflicted wound. Cleopatra has been captured by Caesar who intends to take her to Rome as a prize of battle. There she would be humiliated, tortured, and eventually killed. Rather than face this fate, Cleopatra is determined to kill herself. She acquires small poisonous snakes (asps) to do the deed. With her are her servants Iras and Charmian.

CLEOPATRA:

Show me, my women, like a Queen. Go fetch
My best attires. I am again for Cydnus
To meet Mark Antony ...
Now noble Charmian, we'll dispatch indeed,
And when thou hast done this chare, I'll give thee leave 5
To play till doomsday. Bring our crown and all ...

Enter Clown with basket which contains asps.

He brings me liberty.
My resolution's placed, and I have nothing
Of woman in me. Now from head to foot
I am marble constant. Now the fleeting moon 10
No planet of mine...

Clown leaves basket and exits.

Give me my robe, put on my crown. I have
Immortal longings in me. Now no more
The juice of Egypt's grape shall moist this lip.
Yare, yare, good Iras, quick. Methinks I hear 15
Antony call. I see him rouse himself
To praise my noble act. I hear him mock
The luck of Caesar ... Husband, I come.
Now to that name my courage prove my title!
I am fire and air. My other elements 20
I give to baser life ...

To an asp, which she applies to her breast.

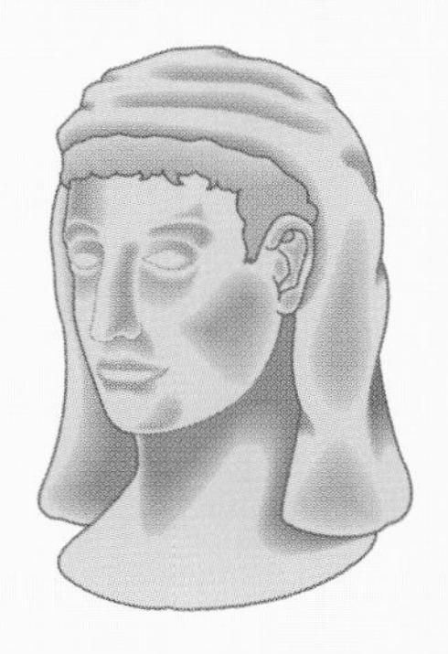

Cleopatra

1. *Show* – present; dress
2. *Cydnus* – the place where she first met and fell in love with Antony
4. *dispatch* – finish our business
5. *chare* – chore; task

10. *fleeting moon* – the moon was considered inconstant because it changed so much

15. *yare* – quickly
18. *luck of Caesar* – Caesar's bad luck because Cleopatra's death will thwart his plans of taking her back as prisoner to Rome
19. "I hope my courageous act proves I deserve to be called your wife."

22. *mortal* – deadly
23. *intrinsicate* – intricate, essential

asp

Come, thou mortal wretch,
With thy sharp teeth this knot intrinsicate
Of life at once untie. Poor venomous fool
Be angry, and dispatch. Peace, peace! ... 25
As sweet as balm, as soft as air, as gentle, —
O Antony! — Nay, I will take thee too.

Applying another asp to her arm.

What should I stay? —

Dies.

Once more unto the breach

(Henry V – Act 3, Scene 1)

King Henry and his troops are about to storm the walls of Harfleur in a critical battle in their campaign against France. The English are badly outnumbered and in need of morale boosting. Before they charge, Henry delivers this memorable pep–talk to his soldiers.

KING HENRY:

Once more unto the breach, dear friends, once more,
Or close the wall up with our English dead.
In peace there's nothing so becomes a man
As modest stillness and humility.
But when the blast of war blows in our ears, 5
Then imitate the action of the tiger.
Stiffen the sinews, conjure up the blood,
Disguise fair nature with hard-favoured rage ...
Now set the teeth and stretch the nostril wide,
Hold hard the breath, and bend up every spirit 10
To his full height. On, on, you noblest English,
Whose blood is fet from fathers of war-proof!
Fathers that, like so many Alexanders,
Have in these parts from morn till even fought,
And sheathed their swords for lack of argument. 15
Dishonour not your mothers. Now attest
That those whom you called fathers did beget you.
Be copy now to men of grosser blood,
And teach them how to war. And you, good yeomen,
Whose limbs were made in England, show us here 20
The mettle of your pasture. Let us swear
That you are worth your breeding, which I doubt not,
For there is none of you so mean and base
That hath not noble lustre in your eyes.
I see you stand like greyhounds in the slips, 25
Straining upon the start. The game's afoot!
Follow your spirit and upon this charge
Cry, "God for Harry, England, and Saint George!"

7. *conjure up* – entreat earnestly
8. *hard-favoured* – grim faced
12. "Whose blood is derived from fathers who have proven themselves in war."
13. *Alexanders* – conquerors
14. *even* – evening
18. *Be copy* – Set an example
18. *grosser* – more common; less knowledgeable
19. *yeomen* – working class
21. *mettle* – quality
23. *mean* – common
25. *slips* – specially designed leashes that allow for easy release in dog races

26. *The game's afoot!*: A line made famous by Sherlock Holmes.

28. *St. George* – patron saint of England

St. George

A good play needs no epilogue

(As You Like It – Epilogue)

In Shakespeare's day, the roles of female characters were played by boys. Here the male actor who plays Rosalind steps out of character, addresses the audience and delivers the epilogue.

4. *bush* – wine makers in Shakespeare's day hung a bush in front of their shops to advertise their products.

10. *insinuate* – ingratiate
12. *conjure* – win over by using magic

17. *simpering* – smirking

20. Remember that, during Shakespeare's day, Rosalind would have been played by a male.

22. *defied* – found objectionable

ROSALIND:

It is not the fashion to see the lady the epilogue,
but it is no more unhandsome than to see the
lord the prologue. If it be true that good wine
needs no bush, 'tis true that a good play needs no
epilogue. 5
Yet to good wine they do use good bushes,
and good plays prove the better by the help
of good epilogues. What a case am I in then,
that am neither a good epilogue, nor cannot
insinuate with you in the behalf of a good play! 10
I am not furnished like a beggar, therefore to beg
will not become me. My way is to conjure you,
and I'll begin with the women. I charge you,
O women, for the love you bear to men,
to like as much of this play as please you. 15
And I charge you, O men, for the love you bear
to women (as I perceive by your simpering,
none of you hates them), that between you
and the women the play may please.
If I were a woman I would kiss as many of you 20
as had beards that pleased me, complexions
that liked me, and breaths that I defied not.
And I am sure, as many as have good beards,
or good faces, or sweet breaths, will for my kind
offer, when I make curtsy, bid me farewell. 25

End of the Unit Activities:

- Choose one of the speeches to memorize and present to the class. Be sure to vary your voice and volume when you deliver your speech. You may also wish to include simple costuming in your presentation.
- Prepare a taped reading or video of your speech with appropriate accompanying music. Create a rock video if you like.
- Rewrite one of the speeches in modern English. Memorize and present it to the class.
- Write a poem or journal entry in response to one of the speeches.
- Create a collage on the ideas or emotions expressed in one of the speeches.

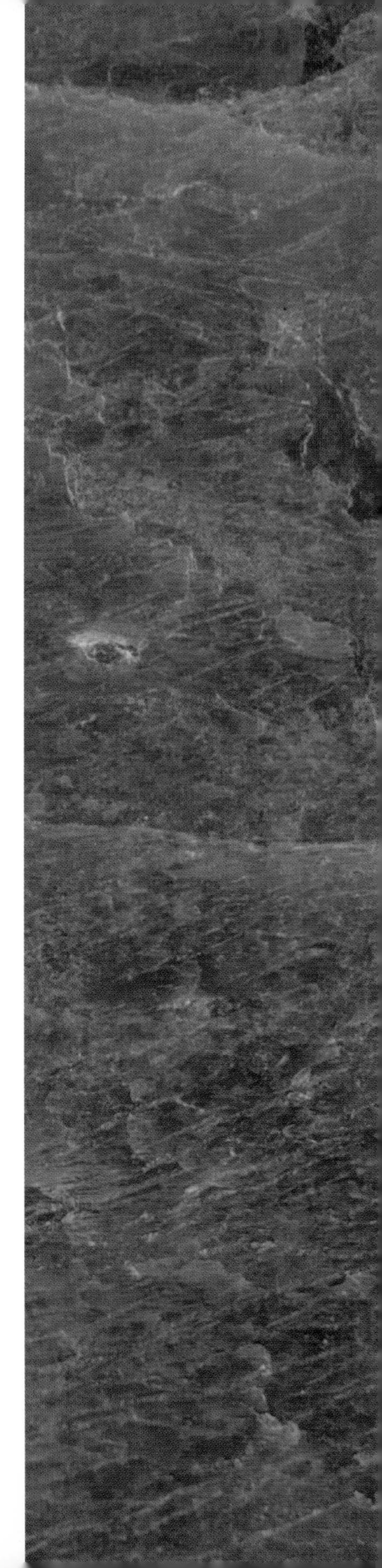

Scenes

Act Two:

"The play's the thing ..."

Everybody loves a spectacle and Shakespeare's plays are frequently nothing less than spectacular. Perhaps this explains why his stories continue to entertain and enthral audiences all over the world. In this unit, you will be introduced to some of Shakespeare's most moving and most amusing scenes.

If you are used to reading modern plays, you will notice immediately that there is quite a difference between these plays and Shakespeare's works. And it's not just in the language.

Modern playwrights are quite generous in providing ample stage directions. This ensures that the author's vision is clear to actors (and readers) and enables them to prepare a production that is faithful to the author's vision—without having to have the author physically present at rehearsals.

Shakespeare, however, used stage directions very sparingly in his plays. Because he was directly involved in the production of the plays, there was little need to record the stage directions. What this means, therefore, is that there is no one correct way to play Shakespeare. You must read the words carefully and sensitively to formulate an interpretation of the text. Then you must translate that interpretation into action and appropriate vocal expression.

As you read these scenes and prepare your presentations, always remember that these words were meant to be spoken aloud and performed with actions. They come from flesh and blood people who express real emotions and who are involved in motivated action. Try to bring out those emotions and motives in your reading and performance.

Hamlet says it best when he advises the actors to "Suit the word to the action, the action to the word."

In this edition, some stage directions are included that did not originally appear in Shakespeare. These are designed to provide some basic information as to what is occurring on stage.

The following stage directions appear frequently in Shakespeare's plays:

Above, aloft – scene is played in the balcony above the stage level or from higher up in the loft

Alarum – a loud shout, a signal call to arms

Aside – speech spoken directly to the audience or to a specified

character and which is not heard by the others on the stage.
Below, beneath – speech or scene played from below the surface of the stage; the actor stands inside an open trap-door.
Exit – he/she leaves the stage
Exeunt – they leave the stage
Flourish – fanfare of trumpets; usually announces the entrance of royalty
Hautboys – musicians enter, playing wind instruments
Omnes – all; everyone
Within – words spoken off-stage in what the audience would assume is an unseen room, corridor, or the outdoors

The Soliloquy:

Another term you should be familiar with is *soliloquy.* Soliloquies are never identified as such in the stage directions but they are easily recognized. They are similar to some *asides* in that they are spoken directly to the audience. The difference lies in the fact that during a soliloquy, the actor is alone on stage. The purpose of the soliloquy is to reveal a character's innermost thoughts or feelings. In thinking aloud, characters also reveal what it is that motivates them and what it is they are planning.

Some of Shakespeare's most famous speeches are soliloquies.

What follows is a series of scenes from Shakespeare's plays. These scenes should serve as a general introduction to what you can expect in a fuller study of a play.

Don't make the mistake of thinking that you need to understand every word and metaphor to appreciate the dramatic value of the scene. As long as you understand most of what is going on in terms of the situation, conflict, and emotions, that is enough. Notes are provided in the margins for the more difficult words in the text.

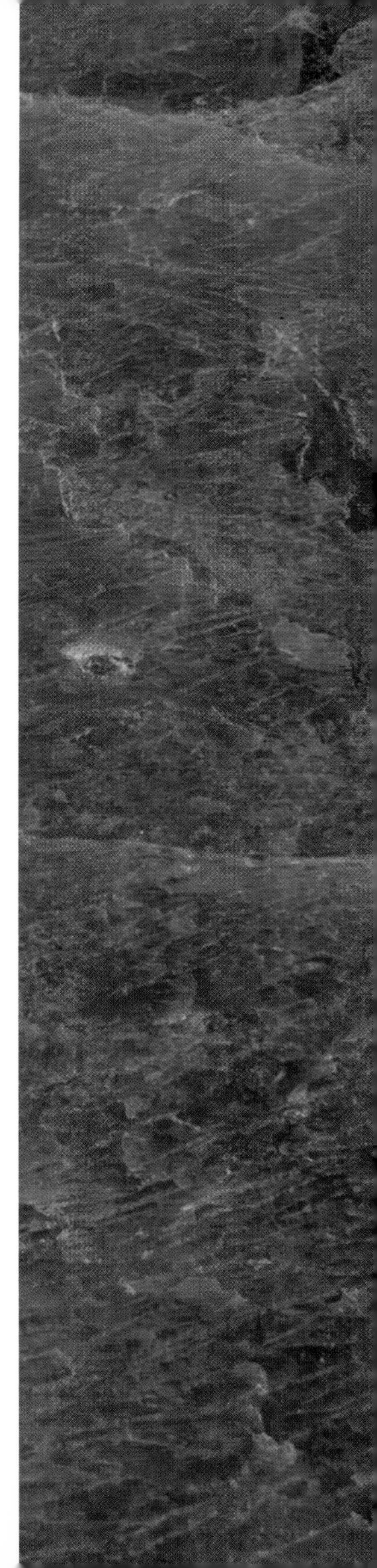

My only love, sprung from my only hate

(Romeo and Juliet – Act 1, Scene 5)

Romeo and his friends (wearing masks to hide their faces) have invited themselves to a party at the Capulets. Romeo sees Juliet and falls instantly in love.

ROMEO: What lady's that, which doth enrich the hand
Of yonder knight?
SERVANT: I know not, sir.
ROMEO: O, she doth teach the torches to burn bright.
It seems she hangs upon the cheek of night 5
Like a rich jewel in an Ethiop's ear –
Beauty too rich for use, for earth too dear.
So shows a snowy dove trooping with crows
As yonder lady over her fellows shows.
The measure done, I'll watch her place of stand 10
And, touching hers, make blessed my rude hand.
Did my heart love till now? Forswear it, sight.
For I never saw true beauty till this night . . .

10. *measure*: dance

12. *forswear*: deny

Romeo makes his way over to Juliet and takes her hand in his.

ROMEO: If I profane with my unworthiest hand
This holy shrine, the gentle sin is this: 15
My lips, two blushing pilgrims, ready stand
To smooth that rough touch with a tender kiss.
JULIET: Good pilgrim, you do wrong your hand too much,
Which mannerly devotion shows in this.
For saints have hands that pilgrims' hands do touch, 20
And palm to palm is holy palmers' kiss.
ROMEO: Have not saints lips, and holy palmers too?
JULIET: Aye, pilgrim, lips that they must use in prayer.
ROMEO: O, then, dear saint, let lips do what hands do.
They pray, grant thou, lest faith turn to despair. 25
JULIET: Saints do not move, though grant for prayers' sake.
ROMEO: Then move not while my prayer's effect I take.

14. *profane*: defile
15. *shrine*: i.e. Juliet's hand
20. *saints*: stone statues of saints
21. *palmers*: pilgrims to the Holy Land carried palm leaves
25. *lest*: for fear that

14 – 27. It is somewhat appropriate that these 14 lines of dialogue, which mark the first meeting between Romeo and Juliet, take the form of a Shakespearean sonnet. See page 85.

He kisses her.

Thus from my lips, by thine, my sin is purged.

28. *purged*: washed clean

JULIET: Then have my lips the sin that they have took.
ROMEO: Sin from my lips? O trespass sweetly urged! 30
Give me my sin again.

He kisses her again.

JULIET: You kiss by the book.
NURSE: Madam, your mother craves a word with you.

Juliet exits.

ROMEO: What is her mother?
NURSE: Marry, bachelor, 35
Her mother is the lady of the house,
And a good lady, and a wise and virtuous.
I nursed her daughter that you talked withal.
I tell you, he that can lay hold of her
Shall have the chinks. 40
ROMEO: Is she a Capulet?
O dear account. My life is my foe's debt ...

Romeo exits. Juliet enters.

JULIET: Come hither, Nurse. What is yond gentleman?
NURSE: The son and heir of old Tiberio.
JULIET: What's he that now is going out of door? 45
NURSE: Marry, that, I think, be young Petruchio.
JULIET: What's he that follows there, that would not dance?
NURSE: I know not.
JULIET: Go ask his name. —

Nurse goes to ask about Romeo and returns immediately.

If he be married,
My grave is like to be my wedding bed. 50
NURSE: His name is Romeo, and a Montague,
The only son of your great enemy.
JULIET: My only love, sprung from my only hate.
Too early seen unknown, and known too late.
Prodigious birth of love it is to me 55
That I must love a loathed enemy.

32. "You kiss as though you had learned your skill from a book."

40. *chinks*: riches; plenty of coin. The word comes from the sound made when coins are rubbed together.

42. *account*: high price to pay

54. "I saw him before I knew who he was and now that I know who he is, it is too late not to fall in love."
55. *prodigious*: ominous

A rose by any other name

(Romeo and Juliet – Act 2, Scene 2)

Romeo, hopelessly in love with Juliet, sneaks into the courtyard of the Capulets. Juliet appears on her balcony and, at first, Romeo remains hidden. What follows may be the most romantic love scene ever written.

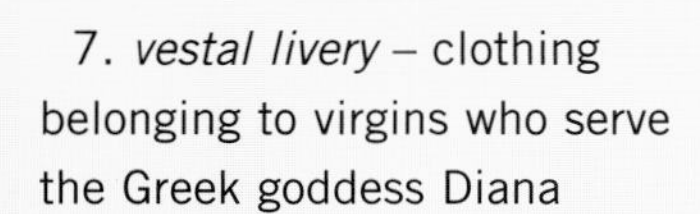

7. *vestal livery* – clothing belonging to virgins who serve the Greek goddess Diana

12. *discourses* – speaks

32. *bestrides* – rides as if on a horse
lazy–puffing – slow moving

34. *wherefore* – why

ROMEO: But soft! What light through yonder window breaks?
It is the east, and Juliet is the sun!
Arise, fair sun, and kill the envious moon,
Who is already sick and pale with grief
That thou her maid art far more fair than she. 5
Be not her maid, since she is envious.
Her vestal livery is but sick and green,
And none but fools do wear it. Cast it off.
It is my lady, O, it is my love!
O that she knew she were! 10
She speaks, yet she says nothing. What of that?
Her eye discourses, I will answer it.
I am too bold. 'Tis not to me she speaks.
Two of the fairest stars in all the heaven,
Having some business, do entreat her eyes 15
To twinkle in their spheres till they return.
What if her eyes were there, they in her head?
The brightness of her cheek would shame those stars
As daylight doth a lamp. Her eyes in heaven
Would through the airy region stream so bright 20
That birds would sing and think it were not night.
See how she leans her cheek upon her hand.
O that I were a glove upon that hand,
That I might touch that cheek!
JULIET: Aye me! 25
ROMEO: She speaks.
O, speak again, bright angel, for thou art
As glorious to this night, being over my head,
As is a winged messenger of heaven
Unto the white-upturned wondering eyes 30
Of mortals that fall back to gaze on him
When he bestrides the lazy-puffing clouds
And sails upon the bosom of the air.
JULIET: O Romeo, Romeo, wherefore art thou Romeo?
Deny thy father and refuse thy name. 35
Or, if thou wilt not, be but sworn my love,
And I'll no longer be a Capulet.

ROMEO: Shall I hear more, or shall I speak at this?
JULIET: 'Tis but thy name that is my enemy.
Thou art thyself, though not a Montague. 40
What's Montague? It is nor hand, nor foot,
Nor arm, nor face, nor any other part
Belonging to a man. O, be some other name.
What's in a name? That which we call a rose
By any other name would smell as sweet. 45
So Romeo would, were he not Romeo called,
Retain that dear perfection which he owes
Without that title. Romeo, doff thy name,
And for that name, which is no part of thee,
Take all myself. 50
ROMEO: I take thee at thy word.
Call me but love, and I'll be new baptized.
Henceforth I never will be Romeo.
JULIET: What man art thou that, thus bescreened in night,
So stumblest on my counsel? 55
ROMEO: By a name
I know not how to tell thee who I am.
My name, dear saint, is hateful to myself,
Because it is an enemy to thee.
Had I it written, I would tear the word. 60
JULIET: My ears have yet not drunk a hundred words
Of that tongue's utterance, yet I know the sound.
Art thou not Romeo, and a Montague?
ROMEO: Neither, fair saint, if either thee dislike.
JULIET: How camest thou hither, tell me, and wherefore? 65
The orchard walls are high and hard to climb,
And the place death, considering who thou art,
If any of my kinsmen find thee here.
ROMEO: With love's light wings did I overperch these walls,
For stony limits cannot hold love out, 70
And what love can do, that dares love attempt.
Therefore thy kinsmen are no stop to me.
JULIET: If they do see thee, they will murder thee.
ROMEO: Alack, there lies more peril in thine eye
Than twenty of their swords! Look thou but sweet, 75
And I am proof against their enmity. . .
JULIET: Dost thou love me? I know thou wilt say 'Aye'
And I will take thy word. Yet, if thou swearest,
Thou mayst prove false . . . O gentle Romeo,
If thou dost love, pronounce it faithfully. 80
Or if thou thinkest I am too quickly won,
I'll frown, and be perverse, and say thee nay,

47. *owes* – possesses
48. *doff* – cast off
55. *counsel* – secrets
69. *overperch* – scale, fly over
72. *stop* – obstacle
76. *proof ... enmity* – protected from their hatred
82. *perverse* – difficult

83. *else* – otherwise

87. *strange* – restrained, distant

89. *ere* – before

91. *impute* – blame

92. *discovered* – revealed

97. *lest* – for fear that

101. *idolatry* – worship

121. *bounty*: generosity

125. *bent*: intention

So thou wilt woo. But else, not for the world.
In truth, fair Montague, I am too fond,
And therefore thou mayst think my haviour light, 85
But trust me, gentleman, I'll prove more true
Than those that have more cunning to be strange.
I should have been more strange, I must confess,
But that thou overheardest, ere I was ware,
My true-love passion. Therefore pardon me, 90
And not impute this yielding to light love,
Which the dark night hath so discovered.

ROMEO: Lady, by yonder blessed moon I vow,
That tips with silver all these fruit-tree tops —

JULIET: O, swear not by the moon, the inconstant moon, 95
That monthly changes in her circled orb,
Lest that thy love prove likewise variable.

ROMEO: What shall I swear by?

JULIET: Do not swear at all;
Or if thou wilt, swear by thy gracious self, 100
Which is the god of my idolatry,
And I'll believe thee.

ROMEO: If my heart's dear love —

JULIET: Well, do not swear. Although I joy in thee,
I have no joy of this contract to-night. 105
It is too rash, too unadvised, too sudden,
Too like the lightning, which doth cease to be
Ere one can say 'It lightens.' Sweet, good night.
This bud of love, by summer's ripening breath,
May prove a beauteous flower when next we meet. 110
Good night, good night. As sweet repose and rest
Come to thy heart as that within my breast.

ROMEO: O, wilt thou leave me so unsatisfied?

JULIET: What satisfaction canst thou have to-night?

ROMEO: The exchange of thy love's faithful vow for mine. 115

JULIET: I gave thee mine before thou didst request it,
And yet I would it were to give again.

ROMEO: Wouldst thou withdraw it? For what purpose, love?

JULIET: But to be frank and give it thee again.
And yet I wish but for the thing I have. 120
My bounty is as boundless as the sea,
My love as deep. The more I give to thee,
The more I have, for both are infinite. . .
Three words, dear Romeo, and good night indeed.
If that thy bent of love be honourable, 125
Thy purpose marriage, send me word to-morrow,
By one that I'll procure to come to thee,

Where and what time thou wilt perform the rite,
And all my fortunes at thy foot I'll lay
And follow thee my lord throughout the world. 130
But if thou meanest not well,
I do beseech thee —
To cease thy suit and leave me to my grief.
To-morrow will I send.

ROMEO: So thrive my soul — 135

JULIET: A thousand times good night! . . .

JULIET: Romeo.

ROMEO: My dear?

JULIET: At what o'clock to-morrow
Shall I send to thee? 140

ROMEO: By the hour of nine.

JULIET: I will not fail. 'Tis twenty years till then.
I have forgot why I did call thee back.

ROMEO: Let me stand here till thou remember it.

JULIET: I shall forget, to have thee still stand there, 145
Remembering how I love thy company.

ROMEO: And I'll still stay, to have thee still forget,
Forgetting any other home but this.

JULIET: 'Tis almost morning. . .
Good night, good night! Parting is such sweet sorrow, 150
That I shall say good night till it be morrow.

ROMEO: Sleep dwell upon thine eyes, peace in thy breast.
Would I were sleep and peace, so sweet to rest.

150. *sweet sorrow* – oxymoron: a literary device that combines two words that are opposite in meaning or effect. One purpose of oxymoron is to convey mixed emotions.

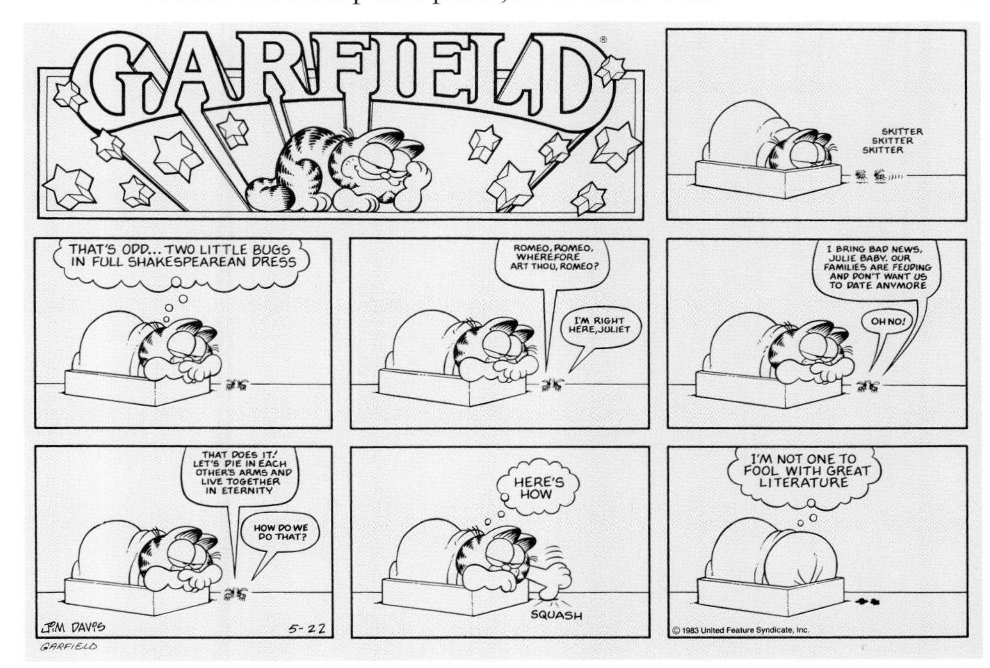

What fire is in mine ears?

(Much Ado About Nothing – Act 3, Scene 1)

Hero and Ursula have decided to play matchmaker with Beatrice, a young lady who has sworn never to marry. Their plan is to get the unsuspecting Beatrice to overhear a conversation during which the two of them will reveal that Benedick, a confirmed bachelor, is in love with her. They hope thereby to plant the seed of love in her.

HERO: Now, Ursula, when Beatrice doth come,
As we do trace this alley up and down,
Our talk must only be of Benedick.
When I do name him, let it be thy part
To praise him more than ever man did merit. 5
My talk to thee must be how Benedick
Is sick in love with Beatrice. Of this matter
Is little Cupid's crafty arrow made,
That only wounds by hearsay. Now begin.

2. *trace* – follow

Enter Beatrice. She notices her friends and hides to overhear the conversation.

For look where Beatrice, like a lapwing runs 10
Close by the ground, to hear our conference.
URSULA: The pleasantest angling is to see the fish
Cut with her golden oars the silver stream,
And greedily devour the treacherous bait.
So angle we for Beatrice, who even now 15
Is couched in the woodbine coverture.
Fear you not my part of the dialogue.
HERO: Then go we near her, that her ear lose nothing
Of the false sweet bait that we lay for it.

10. *lapwing* – a bird, similar to the partridge, that scampers quickly close to the ground
12. *angling* – fishing
13. *oars* – fins
16. *woodbine coverture* – honeysuckle bushes

Finally Beatrice approaches the bower where her friends are seated pretending to have a serious heated discussion. Beatrice remains hidden throughout, but she and her reactions to what she hears are visible to the audience.

No, truly, Ursula, she is too disdainful. 20
I know her spirits are as coy and wild
As haggards of the rock.

20. *disdainful*: proud
21. *coy*: unapproachable; inaccessible
22. *haggards*: hawks

URSULA: But are you sure
That Benedick loves Beatrice so entirely?
HERO: So says the prince and my new-trothed lord. 25
URSULA: And did they bid you tell her of it, madam?
HERO: They did entreat me to acquaint her of it.
But I persuaded them, if they loved Benedick,
To wish him wrestle with affection,
And never to let Beatrice know of it. 30
URSULA: Why did you so? Doth not the gentleman
Deserve as full as fortunate a bed
As ever Beatrice shall couch upon?
HERO: O god of love! I know he doth deserve
As much as may be yielded to a man. 35
But Nature never framed a woman's heart
Of prouder stuff than that of Beatrice.
Disdain and scorn ride sparkling in her eyes,
Misprising what they look on, and her wit
Values itself so highly that to her 40
All matter else seems weak. She cannot love,
Nor take no shape nor project of affection,
She is so self-endeared.
URSULA: Sure, I think so
And therefore certainly it were not good 45
She knew his love, lest she make sport at it.
HERO: Why, you speak truth. I never yet saw man,
How wise, how noble, young, how rarely featured,
But she would spell him backward. If fair-faced,
She would swear the gentleman should be her sister... 50
If tall, a lance ill-headed.
If low, an agate very vilely cut.
If speaking, why, a vane blown with all winds.
If silent, why, a block moved with none.
So turns she every man the wrong side out 55
And never gives to truth and virtue that
Which simpleness and merit purchaseth.
URSULA: Sure, sure, such carping is not commendable.
HERO: No, not to be so odd and from all fashions
As Beatrice is, cannot be commendable. 60
But who dare tell her so? If I should speak,
She would mock me into air. O, she would laugh me
Out of myself, press me to death with wit.
Therefore let Benedick, like covered fire,
Consume away in sighs, waste inwardly. 65
It were a better death than die with mocks,
Which is as bad as die with tickling.

25. *new-trothed* – newly betrothed

29. *wrestle with* – fight, hold back

39. *misprising* – scorning

43. *self-endeared* – in love with herself

46. *lest* – for fear that

49. *spell him backward* – turn him inside out

52. *agate* – semi-precious stone

57. *simpleness* – honesty
purchaseth – deserves

URSULA: Yet tell her of it. Hear what she will say.
HERO: No. Rather I will go to Benedick
And counsel him to fight against his passion. 70
And, truly, I'll devise some honest slanders
To stain my cousin with. One doth not know
How much an ill word may empoison liking.
URSULA: O, do not do your cousin such a wrong.
She cannot be so much without true judgment— 75
Having so swift and excellent a wit
As she is prized to have—as to refuse
So rare a gentleman as Signior Benedick.
HERO: He is the only man of Italy.
Always excepted my dear Claudio. 80
URSULA: I pray you, be not angry with me, madam,
Speaking my fancy. Signior Benedick,
For shape, for bearing, argument and valour,
Goes foremost in report through Italy.
HERO: Indeed, he hath an excellent good name. 85
URSULA: His excellence did earn it, ere he had it.
When are you married, madam?
HERO: Why, every day, to-morrow. Come, go in.
I'll show thee some attires, and have thy counsel
Which is the best to furnish me to-morrow. 90

Hero and Ursula walk away from where Beatrice can hear them.

URSULA: She's limed, I warrant you.
We have caught her, madam.
HERO: If it proves so, then loving goes by haps.
Some Cupid kills with arrows, some with traps.

Hero and Ursula exit leaving behind a puzzled Beatrice. She comes forward and addresses the audience.

BEATRICE: What fire is in mine ears? Can this be true? 95
Stand I condemned for pride and scorn so much?
Contempt, farewell! And maiden pride, adieu!
No glory lives behind the back of such.
And, Benedick, love on. I will requite thee,
Taming my wild heart to thy loving hand. 100
If thou dost love, my kindness shall incite thee
To bind our loves up in a holy band.
For others say thou dost deserve, and I
Believe it better than reportingly.

79. *only* – foremost; best
80. *Always excepted* – With the exception of
82. *Speaking my fancy* – for expressing what's on my mind
86. *ere* – before
88. *every day, to-morrow* – i.e. tomorrow and every day thereafter
91. *limed* – caught, trapped
warrant – guarantee

In the previous scene, the same trick was pulled successfully on Benedick by his friends.

99. *requite* – repay
104. *reportingly* – as it is reported

Will you, nill you, I will marry you

(The Taming of the Shrew – Act 2, Scene 1)

Petruchio, in his pursuit of a wife with a large dowry, has been given permission to woo Katherine. Katherine, however, has the reputation of being a shrew — a woman who is not easy to get along with — to say the least. Petruchio is determined to marry Katherine and will go to any length to get his way.

PETRUCHIO: Good morrow, Kate, for that's your name, I hear.
KATHERINE: Well have you heard, but something hard of
hearing.
They call me Katherine that do talk of me.
PETRUCHIO: You lie, in faith, for you are called plain Kate, 5
And bonny Kate and sometimes Kate the curst,
But Kate, the prettiest Kate in Christendom
Kate of Kate Hall, my super-dainty Kate,
For dainties are all Kates, and therefore, Kate,
Take this of me, Kate of my consolation. 10
Hearing thy mildness praised in every town,
Thy virtues spoke of, and thy beauty sounded,
Yet not so deeply as to thee belongs,
Myself am moved to woo thee for my wife.
KATHERINE: Moved! In good time. 15
Let him that moved you hither
Remove you hence. I knew you at the first
You were a moveable.
PETRUCHIO: Why, what's a moveable?
KATHERINE: A joined-stool. 20
PETRUCHIO: Thou hast hit it. Come, sit on me.

Forces her to sit on his lap.

KATHERINE: Asses are made to bear, and so are you.
PETRUCHIO: Women are made to bear, and so are you.
KATHERINE: No such jade as you, if me you mean.
PETRUCHIO: Alas, Good Kate, I will not burden thee, 25
For, knowing thee to be but young and light—
KATHERINE: Too light for such a swain as you to catch,
And yet as heavy as my weight should be.
PETRUCHIO: Should be! Should—buzz!

6. *curst* – ill-tempered; difficult to get along with

9. *dainties* – delicacies. A pun: another word for dainties is *cates.*

12. *sounded* – measured for depth; mentioned

18. *moveable* – a piece of furniture

20. *joined-stool* – foldable stool

24. *jade* – worthless horse

27. *swain* – naive suitor

29. Petruchio puns on *bees* and the sound they make.

31. *turtle* – i.e. turtle-dove

44. *try* – test

46 – 48. Katherine's puns depend on the fact that gentlemen were entitled to a coat of arms. If he strikes her, he is no gentleman and he will lose his (coat of) arms.

51. *crab* – i.e. crab apple

55. *glass* – mirror; looking-glass

62. *sooth* – truth

63. *chafe* – irritate
tarry – stay

67. *gamesome* – playful

69. *askance* – sideways (in scorn)

71. *cross* – confrontational

KATHERINE: Well taken, and like a buzzard. 30
PETRUCHIO: O slow-winged turtle! Shall a buzzard take thee?
KATHERINE: Ay, for a turtle, as he takes a buzzard.
PETRUCHIO: Come, come, you wasp.
In faith, you are too angry.
KATHERINE: If I be waspish, best beware my sting. 35
PETRUCHIO: My remedy is then, to pluck it out.
KATHERINE: Ay, if the fool could find it where it lies.
PETRUCHIO: Who knows not where a wasp does
wear his sting? In his tail.
KATHERINE: In his tongue. 40
PETRUCHIO: Whose tongue?
KATHERINE: Yours, if you talk of tails, and so farewell ...
PETRUCHIO: Good Kate, I am a gentleman.
KATHERINE: That I'll try.

She strikes him.

PETRUCHIO: I swear I'll cuff you, if you strike again. 45
KATHERINE: So may you lose your arms.
If you strike me, you are no gentleman
And if no gentleman, why then no arms ...
PETRUCHIO: Nay, come, Kate, come.
You must not look so sour. 50
KATHERINE: It is my fashion, when I see a crab.
PETRUCHIO: Why, here's no crab and therefore look not sour.
KATHERINE: There is, there is.
PETRUCHIO: Then show it me.
KATHERINE: Had I a glass, I would. 55
PETRUCHIO: What, you mean my face?
KATHERINE: Well aimed of such a young one.
PETRUCHIO: Now, by Saint George, I am too young for you.
KATHERINE: Yet you are withered.
PETRUCHIO: 'Tis with cares. 60
KATHERINE: I care not.
PETRUCHIO: Nay, hear you, Kate. In sooth you scape not so.
KATHERINE: I chafe you, if I tarry. Let me go.
PETRUCHIO: No, not a whit. I find you passing gentle.
'Twas told me you were rough and coy and sullen, 65
And now I find report a very liar,
For thou are pleasant, gamesome, passing courteous,
But slow in speech, yet sweet as spring-time flowers.
Thou canst not frown, thou canst not look askance,
Nor bite the lip, as angry wenches will, 70
Nor hast thou pleasure to be cross in talk,

But thou with mildness entertainest thy wooers,
With gentle conference, soft and affable ...

KATHERINE: Where did you study all this goodly speech?

PETRUCHIO: It is extempore, from my mother-wit. 75

KATHERINE: A witty mother! Witless else her son ...

PETRUCHIO: Thus in plain terms, your father hath consented
That you shall be my wife. Your dowry agreed on,
And, will you, nill you, I will marry you.
Now, Kate, I am a husband for your turn, 80
For, by this light, whereby I see thy beauty,
Thy beauty, that doth make me like thee well,
Thou must be married to no man but me,
For I am he am born to tame you Kate,
And bring you from a wild Kate to a Kate 85
Conformable as other household Kates.
Here comes your father. Never make denial.
I must and will have Katherine to my wife.

73. *conference* – conversation

75. *mother-wit* – natural-born intelligence

79. *will you, nill you* – whether you will it or not

80. *for your turn* – just right for you

85. *Kate* – here Petruchio puns on Kate and cat

Out of this wood do not desire to go

(A Midsummer Night's Dream – Act 3, Scene 1)

This scene takes place in a magical forest inhabited by fairies. Bottom, a human, now sports the head of an ass on his shoulders but he is not aware of the transformation. His friends, horrified at his monstrous appearance, have abandoned him. Titania, Queen of the Fairies, has been placed under a magical spell while sleeping. When she wakes, she will fall madly in love with the first living thing she sees.

1. *knavery* – treachery

Remember that Bottom is not aware that he has been transformed and that his head has been replaced by the head of a jackass. His lines are ironic to say the least.

5. *ousel cock* – male blackbird

15. *set his wit to* – argue with

17. *never so* – ever so much

21. *perforce* – of necessity

27. *gleek* – make a joke

BOTTOM: I see their knavery. This is to make an ass of me—
to fright me, if they could. But I will not stir from this place,
do what they can. I will walk up and down here, and I will
sing, that they shall hear I am not afraid.
[Sings.] The ousel cock so black of hue, 5
With orange-tawny bill,
The throstle with his note so true,
The wren with little quill,
TITANIA: *[Awaking]* What angel wakes me from my
flowery bed? 10
BOTTOM:
[Sings.] The finch, the sparrow and the lark,
The plain-song cuckoo gray,
Whose note full many a man doth mark,
And dares not answer nay;—
for, indeed, who would set his wit to so foolish 15
a bird? Who would give a bird the lie, though he cry
'cuckoo' never so?
TITANIA: I pray thee, gentle mortal, sing again.
Mine ear is much enamoured of thy note.
So is mine eye enthralled to thy shape, 20
And thy fair virtue's force perforce doth move me
On the first view to say, to swear, I love thee.
BOTTOM: Methinks, mistress, you should have little reason
for that and yet, to say the truth, reason and
love keep little company together now-a-days. The 25
more the pity that some honest neighbours will not
make them friends. Nay, I can gleek upon occasion.

TITANIA: Thou art as wise as thou art beautiful.
BOTTOM: Not so, neither. But if I had wit enough to get out
of this wood, I have enough to serve mine own turn. 30
TITANIA: Out of this wood do not desire to go.
Thou shalt remain here, whether thou wilt or no.
I am a spirit of no common rate.
The summer still doth tend upon my state
And I do love thee. Therefore, go with me. 35
I'll give thee fairies to attend on thee,
And they shall fetch thee jewels from the deep,
And sing while thou on pressed flowers dost sleep.
And I will purge thy mortal grossness so
That thou shalt like an airy spirit go. 40
Peaseblossom! Cobweb! Moth! And Mustardseed!

Enter Peaseblossom, Cobweb, Moth, and Mustardseed.

PEASEBLOSSOM: Ready.
COBWEB: And I.
MOTH: And I.
MUSTARDSEED: And I. 45
ALL: Where shall we go?
TITANIA: Be kind and courteous to this gentleman.
Hop in his walks and gambol in his eyes.
Feed him with apricocks and dewberries,
With purple grapes, green figs, and mulberries. 50
The honey-bags steal from the humble-bees,
And for night-tapers crop their waxen thighs
And light them at the fiery glow-worm's eyes,
To have my love to bed and to arise.
And pluck the wings from painted butterflies 55
To fan the moonbeams from his sleeping eyes.
Nod to him, elves, and do him courtesies.
PEASEBLOSSOM: Hail, mortal!
COBWEB: Hail!
MOTH: Hail! 60
MUSTARDSEED: Hail!
BOTTOM: I cry your worship's mercy, heartily.
I beseech your worship's name.
COBWEB: Cobweb.
BOTTOM: I shall desire you of more acquaintance, good 65
Master Cobweb. If I cut my finger, I shall make bold
with you. Your name, honest gentleman?
PEASEBLOSSOM: Peaseblossom.

33. *rate*: rank
34. *still doth tend*: always attends or depends. Titania's power controls the seasons.

39 – 40. Titania offers to make Bottom an immortal like herself.

48. *gambol*: leap, dance

52. *night-tapers*: candles

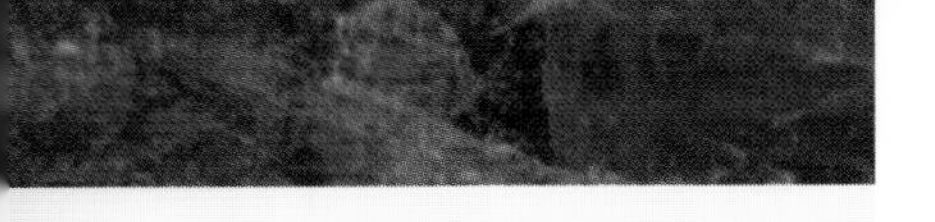

70. *Peascod* – a ripe pea-pod

BOTTOM: I pray you, commend me to Mistress Squash,
your mother, and to Master Peascod, your father. 70
Good Master Peaseblossom, I shall desire you of more
acquaintance too. Your name, I beseech you, sir?

MUSTARDSEED: Mustardseed.

BOTTOM: Good Master Mustardseed, I know your patience
well. That same cowardly, giant-like ox-beef hath 75
devoured many a gentleman of your house. I promise
you your kindred had made my eyes water ere now.
I desire your more acquaintance, good Master
Mustardseed.

77. *ere* – before

TITANIA: Come, wait upon him. Lead him to my bower. 80
The moon methinks, looks like a watery eye,
And when she weeps, weeps every little flower,
Lamenting some enforced chastity.
Tie up my love's tongue, bring him silently.

81 – 3. A reference to dew on the flowers. It was believed that dew came down from the moon.

I'll put another question to thee

(Hamlet – Act 5, Scene 1)

Both roles in this scene would have been played by the clowns in Shakespeare's company.

As a grave-digger goes about his trade, he converses with a friend and challenges him with a riddle.

GRAVE-DIGGER: Come, my spade. There is no ancient
gentleman but gardeners, ditchers, and grave-makers—
they hold up Adam's profession.
OTHER: Was he a gentleman?
GRAVE-DIGGER: He was the first that ever bore arms. 5
OTHER: Why, he had none.
GRAVE-DIGGER: What, art a heathen?
How dost thou understand the Scripture? The Scripture says
Adam digged. Could he dig without arms? I'll put another
question to thee. If thou answerest me not to the 10
purpose, confess thyself—
OTHER: Go to.
GRAVE-DIGGER: What is he that builds stronger than either the
mason, the shipwright, or the carpenter?
OTHER: The gallows-maker, for that frame outlives a 15
thousand tenants.
GRAVE-DIGGER: I like thy wit well, in good faith. The gallows
does well. But how does it well? It does well to those that do
ill. Now thou dost ill to say the gallows is built stronger
than the church. Argal, the gallows may do well to thee. 20
To it again, come.
OTHER: Who builds stronger than a mason, a shipwright,
or a carpenter?
GRAVE-DIGGER: Ay, tell me that, and unyoke.
OTHER: Marry, now I can tell. 25
GRAVE-DIGGER: To it.
OTHER: Mass, I cannot tell.
GRAVE-DIGGER: Cudgel thy brains no more about it, ...
And when you are asked this question next, say 'A grave-
maker.' The houses he makes last till doomsday. 30
Go, get thee to Yaughan. Fetch me a stoup of liquor.

3. *Adam's profession* – out of necessity, Adam became a farmer or gardener – one who digs the earth

5. *bore arms* – pun on "coat of arms" that gentlemen were entitled to bear.

20. *argal*: i.e. ergo – therefore

24. *unyoke* – have done with it (as when an ox is finished with his toil)

28. *cudgel*: beat (with a stick)

31. *Yaughan* – perhaps the name of a local inn-keeper.

Take away the fool

(Twelfth Night – Act 1, Scene 5)

6. *fear no colours* – i.e., fear no enemy colours or flags. There is also a pun on *collars* – hangman's noose

colours

8. *to be turned away* – fired from the position

11. *and it* – if it
12. *Those wits* – those so-called intelligent persons (who think they are witty)
14. *Quinapalus* – an impressive sounding name which the Clown has made up

19. *dry* – lacking wit; boring

25. *botcher*: a tailor who mends clothes but not well

Feste the Clown has been absent from his post without permission but has now returned. The Lady Olivia is still in mourning over the death of her brother and is in no mood to tolerate the attempts of the Clown to cheer her up. Nevertheless the Clown must try even though he may be punished for it.

Enter Maria and Clown Feste.

MARIA: Nay, either tell me where thou hast been, or
I will not open my lips so wide as a bristle may enter,
in way of thy excuse. My lady will hang thee for
thy absence.
CLOWN: Let her hang me! He that is well hanged in 5
this world needs to fear no colours ...
MARIA: Yet you will be hang'd for being so long
absent, or to be turned away — is not that as good as a
hanging to you? ... Here comes my lady.
Make your excuse wisely, you were best. 10

Exit Maria.

CLOWN: Wit, and it be thy will, put me into good fooling!
Those wits that think they have thee do very oft prove
fools, and I that am sure I lack thee, may pass for a
wise man. For what says Quinapalus? "Better a witty
fool than a foolish wit." 15

Enter Lady Olivia with Attendants.

God bless thee, lady!
OLIVIA: Take the fool away.
CLOWN: Do you not hear, fellows? Take away the lady.
OLIVIA: Go to, you are a dry fool. I'll no more of you.
Besides, you grow dishonest. 20
CLOWN: Two faults, madonna, that drink and good counsel
will amend; for give the dry fool drink, then is the
fool not dry. Bid the dishonest man mend himself:
if he mend, he is no longer dishonest; if he cannot, let
the botcher mend him ... The lady bade take away the 25
fool, therefore I say again, take her away.

OLIVIA: Sir, I bade them take away you.
CLOWN: Misprision in the highest degree! ... Good madonna, give me leave to prove you a fool.
OLIVIA: Can you do it? 30
CLOWN: Dexteriously, good madonna.
OLIVIA: Make your proof.
CLOWN: I must catechize you for it, madonna. Good my mouse of virtue, answer me.
OLIVIA: Well, sir, for want of other idleness, I'll bide your proof. 35
CLOWN: Good madonna, why mournest thou?
OLIVIA: Good fool, for my brother's death.
CLOWN: I think his soul is in hell, madonna.
OLIVIA: I know his soul is in heaven, fool. 40
CLOWN: The more fool, madonna, to mourn for your brother's soul, being in heaven. Take away the fool, gentlemen.

28. *Misprision* – misunderstanding; gross error
29. *leave* – permission

33. *catechize* – question formally
34. *mouse of virtue* – playful term of affection
35. *bide*: wait for

Conrad **by R. Scholz**

Double, double, toil and trouble

(Macbeth – Act 4, Scene 1)

Three witches prepare a spell in anticipation of Macbeth's arrival. They had correctly predicted that Macbeth would be King of Scotland. Now he seeks them out to get more information concerning his fate.

FIRST WITCH: Thrice the brinded cat hath mewed.
SECOND WITCH: Thrice and once the hedge-pig whined.
THIRD WITCH: Harpier cries, "'Tis time, 'tis time."
FIRST WITCH: Round about the cauldron go;
In the poisoned entrails throw. 5
Toad, that under cold stone
Days and nights has thirty-one
Sweltered venom sleeping got,
Boil thou first in the charmed pot.
ALL: Double, double, toil and trouble, 10
Fire burn and cauldron bubble.
SECOND WITCH: Fillet of a fenny snake,
In the cauldron boil and bake.
Eye of newt and toe of frog,
Wool of bat and tongue of dog, 15
Adder's fork and blind-worm's sting,
Lizard's leg and howlet's wing,
For a charm of powerful trouble,
Like a hell-broth boil and bubble.
ALL: Double, double, toil and trouble, 20
Fire burn and cauldron bubble.
THIRD WITCH: Scale of dragon, tooth of wolf,
Witch's mummy, maw and gulf
Of the ravined salt-sea shark,
Root of hemlock digged in the dark, 25
Liver of blaspheming Jew,
Gall of goat and slips of yew
Slivered in the moon's eclipse,
Nose of Turk and Tartar's lips,
Finger of birth-strangled babe 30
Ditch-delivered by a drab,
Make the gruel thick and slab.
Add thereto a tiger's chaudron,
For the ingredients of our cauldron.

1. *brinded* – streaked
2. *hedge-pig* – hedgehog

12. *fenny* – from the marshes

16. *fork* – forked tongue
blind-worm – small lizard
17. *howlet* – small owl

23. *maw and gulf* – stomach and gullet
24. *ravined* – ravenous

27. *yew* – a tree that was commonly found in church-yards. The entire tree was considered poisonous.

29. Turks and Tartars were considered unbaptized and therefore valued by the witches.

31. *drab* – prostitute
33. *chaudron* – entrails

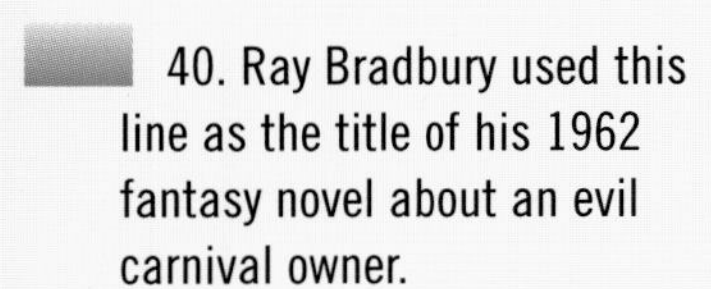

40. Ray Bradbury used this line as the title of his 1962 fantasy novel about an evil carnival owner.

ALL: Double, double, toil and trouble, 35
Fire burn and cauldron bubble.
SECOND WITCH: Cool it with a baboon's blood,
Then the charm is firm and good.
THIRD WITCH: By the pricking of my thumbs,
Something wicked this way comes. 40
Open, locks, whoever knocks!

Enter Macbeth.

MACBETH: How now, you secret, black, and midnight hags?
What is it you do?
ALL: A deed without a name.
MACBETH: I conjure you, by that which you profess, 45
However you come to know it, answer me. . .
FIRST WITCH: Speak.
SECOND WITCH: Demand.
THIRD WITCH: We'll answer.

Caesar shall go forth

(Julius Caesar – Act 2, Scene 2)

Caesar has been forewarned to "Beware the Ides of March." That day has come and thunder and lightning can be heard. Caesar's wife has had bad dreams and she fears her husband will come to harm.

Enter Caesar, still in his night-gown.

CAESAR: Nor heaven nor earth have been at peace to-night.
Thrice hath Calpurnia in her sleep cried out,
'Help, ho! They murder Caesar!' Who's within?

Enter a Servant.

SERVANT: My lord?
CAESAR: Go bid the priests do present sacrifice 5
And bring me their opinions of success.
SERVANT: I will, my lord.

The servant exits. Caesar's wife, Calpurnia, enters.

CALPURNIA: What mean you, Caesar?
Think you to walk forth?
You shall not stir out of your house to-day. 10
CAESAR: Caesar shall forth. The things that threatened me
Never looked but on my back. When they shall see
The face of Caesar, they are vanished.
CALPURNIA: Caesar, I never stood on ceremonies,
Yet now they fright me. There is one within, 15
Besides the things that we have heard and seen,
Recounts most horrid sights seen by the watch.
A lioness hath whelped in the streets,
And graves have yawned, and yielded up their dead.
Fierce fiery warriors fought upon the clouds, 20
In ranks and squadrons and right form of war,
Which drizzled blood upon the Capitol.
The noise of battle hurtled in the air,
Horses did neigh, and dying men did groan,
And ghosts did shriek and squeal about the streets. 25
O Caesar! These things are beyond all use,
And I do fear them.
CAESAR: What can be avoided
Whose end is purposed by the mighty gods?
Yet Caesar shall go forth, for these predictions 30

Julius Caesar

11 – 13. Caesar is a true tragic hero in that he suffers from what the Greeks called *hubris* – excess pride or will. It is the confidence that people have when they feel they cannot be stopped, beaten or affected by anything around them. When combined with a bad choice, *hubris* sometimes leads to tragedy.

18. *whelped* – given birth
19. *yawned* – opened up

26. *beyond all use* – outside of common experience

32 – 33. Calpurnia here expresses a common view held by the Elizabethans that nature reflects and parallels what is occurring in the lives of people. The unnatural events of the evening described in lines 15 – 26 are explained by the fact that, during the night, a group of conspirators were plotting to kill Caesar. Plotting to kill a ruler or king was considered the most unnatural act of all.

33. *blaze forth* – announce
40. *augurers* – fortune tellers

53. Calpurnia here comments on Caesar's *hubris.* See note for lines 11–13.

Are to the world in general as to Caesar.
CALPURNIA: When beggars die, there are no comets seen.
The heavens themselves blaze forth the death of princes.
CAESAR: Cowards die many times before their deaths —
The valiant never taste of death but once. 35
Of all the wonders that I yet have heard,
It seems to me most strange that men should fear,
Seeing that death, a necessary end,
Will come when it will come.

Re-enter Servant.

What say the augurers? 40
SERVANT: They would not have you to stir forth to-day.
Plucking the entrails of an offering forth,
They could not find a heart within the beast.
CAESAR: The gods do this in shame of cowardice.
Caesar should be a beast without a heart, 45
If he should stay at home to-day for fear.
No, Caesar shall not. Danger knows full well
That Caesar is more dangerous than he.
We are two lions littered in one day,
And I the elder and more terrible, 50
And Caesar shall go forth.
CALPURNIA: Alas, my lord,
Your wisdom is consumed in confidence.
Do not go forth to-day. Call it my fear
That keeps you in the house and not your own. 55
We'll send Mark Antony to the senate-house
And he shall say you are not well to-day.
Let me, upon my knee, prevail in this.
CAESAR: Mark Antony shall say I am not well,
And, for thy humour, I will stay at home. 60

Enter Decius Brutus.

Here's Decius Brutus, he shall tell them so.
DECIUS: Caesar, all hail!
Good morrow, worthy Caesar.
I come to fetch you to the senate-house.
CAESAR: And you are come in very happy time 65
To bear my greeting to the senators
And tell them that I will not come to-day.
Cannot, is false, and that I dare not, falser.
I will not come to-day. Tell them so, Decius.

CALPURNIA: Say he is sick. 70
CAESAR: Shall Caesar send a lie?
Have I in conquest stretched mine arm so far
To be afraid to tell graybeards the truth?
Decius, go tell them Caesar will not come.
DECIUS: Most mighty Caesar, 75
Let me know some cause,
Lest I be laughed at when I tell them so.
CAESAR: The cause is in my will — I will not come.
That is enough to satisfy the senate.
But for your private satisfaction, 80
Because I love you, I will let you know.
Calpurnia here, my wife, stays me at home.
She dreamt to-night she saw my statue,
Which, like a fountain with an hundred spouts,
Did run pure blood, and many lusty Romans 85
Came smiling, and did bathe their hands in it.
And these does she apply for warnings, and portents,
And evils imminent. And on her knee
Hath begged that I will stay at home to-day.
DECIUS: This dream is all amiss interpreted. 90
It was a vision fair and fortunate.
Your statue spouting blood in many pipes,
In which so many smiling Romans bathed,
Signifies that from you great Rome shall suck
Reviving blood, and that great men shall press 95
For tinctures, stains, relics and cognizance.
This by Calpurnia's dream is signified.
CAESAR: And this way have you well expounded it.
DECIUS: I have, when you have heard what I can say
And know it now. The senate have concluded 100
To give this day a crown to mighty Caesar.
If you shall send them word you will not come,
Their minds may change. Besides, it were a mock
Apt to be rendered, for some one to say
'Break up the senate till another time, 105
When Caesar's wife shall meet with better dreams.'
If Caesar hide himself, shall they not whisper
'Lo, Caesar is afraid'?
Pardon me, Caesar, for my dear dear love
To your proceeding bids me tell you this 110
And reason to my love is liable.
CAESAR: How foolish do your fears seem now, Calpurnia!
I am ashamed I did yield to them.
Give me my robe, for I will go.

77. *lest* – for fear that

82. *stays* – keeps

87. *portents* – signs

96. Decius here refers to the common practice of people dipping their handkerchiefs in the blood of martyrs and keeping the bloody napkins as remembrances of the martyr.

110. *proceeding* – advancement

111. "My love for you is stronger than my better judgment."

Friends, Romans, countrymen

(Julius Caesar – Act 3, Scene 2)

Julius Caesar has just been assassinated and his closest friend, Mark Antony has been given permission by the killers to speak to the Roman crowd at Caesar's funeral

4. *interred* – buried

Antony is very careful when he begins his oration. The crowd is pro-Brutus and will not tolerate anything negative being said about him. Antony works at the crowd slowly and gets them to realize that if Brutus was wrong in one thing (claiming that Caesar was ambitious), then Brutus could also have been wrong in killing Caesar. Antony is a master manipulator. Watch him as he works the mob and uses them for his own purposes – the utter destruction of the conspirators who killed Caesar.

23. *Lupercal* – spring festival to commemorate the suckling of Rome's founders, Romulus and Remus, by a wolf.

Romulus & Remus

ANTONY: Friends, Romans, countrymen, lend me your ears.
I come to bury Caesar, not to praise him.
The evil that men do lives after them,
The good is oft interred with their bones.
So let it be with Caesar. The noble Brutus 5
Hath told you Caesar was ambitious.
If it were so, it was a grievous fault,
And grievously hath Caesar answered it.
Here, under leave of Brutus and the rest—
For Brutus is an honourable man, 10
So are they all, all honourable men—
Come I to speak in Caesar's funeral.
He was my friend, faithful and just to me.
But Brutus says he was ambitious,
And Brutus is an honourable man. 15
He hath brought many captives home to Rome
Whose ransoms did the general coffers fill.
Did this in Caesar seem ambitious?
When that the poor have cried, Caesar hath wept.
Ambition should be made of sterner stuff. 20
Yet Brutus says he was ambitious,
And Brutus is an honourable man.
You all did see that on the Lupercal
I thrice presented him a kingly crown,
Which he did thrice refuse. Was this ambition? 25
Yet Brutus says he was ambitious,
And, sure, he is an honourable man.
I speak not to disprove what Brutus spoke,
But here I am to speak what I do know.
You all did love him once, not without cause. 30
What cause withholds you then, to mourn for him?
O judgment! Thou art fled to brutish beasts,
And men have lost their reason. Bear with me.
My heart is in the coffin there with Caesar,
And I must pause till it come back to me. 35

FIRST CITIZEN: Methinks there is much reason in his sayings.
SECOND CITIZEN: If thou consider rightly of the matter,
Caesar has had great wrong.
THIRD CITIZEN: Has he, masters?
I fear there will a worse come in his place. 40
FOURTH CITIZEN: Marked ye his words?
He would not take the crown.
Therefore 'tis certain he was not ambitious.
FIRST CITIZEN: If it be found so, some will dear abide it.
SECOND CITIZEN: Poor soul! His eyes are red as fire 45
with weeping.
THIRD CITIZEN: There's not a nobler man in Rome
than Antony.
FOURTH CITIZEN: Now mark him, he begins again to speak.
ANTONY: But yesterday the word of Caesar might 50
Have stood against the world — now lies he there.
And none so poor to do him reverence.
O masters, if I were disposed to stir
Your hearts and minds to mutiny and rage,
I should do Brutus wrong, and Cassius wrong, 55
Who, you all know, are honourable men.
I will not do them wrong. I rather choose
To wrong the dead, to wrong myself and you,
Than I will wrong such honourable men.
But here's a parchment with the seal of Caesar. 60
I found it in his closet, 'tis his will.
Let but the commons hear this testament—
Which, pardon me, I do not mean to read—
And they would go and kiss dead Caesar's wounds
And dip their napkins in his sacred blood ... 65
FOURTH CITIZEN: We'll hear the will! Read it, Mark Antony.
ALL: The will, the will! We will hear Caesar's will.
ANTONY: Have patience, gentle friends, I must not read it.
It is not meet you know how Caesar loved you.
You are not wood, you are not stones, ... 70
It will inflame you, it will make you mad:
'Tis good you know not that you are his heirs.
For, if you should, O, what would come of it!
FOURTH CITIZEN: Read the will! We'll hear it, Antony!
You shall read us the will, Caesar's will. 75
ANTONY: Will you be patient? Will you stay awhile? ...
I fear I wrong the honourable men
Whose daggers have stabbed Caesar. I do fear it.
FOURTH CITIZEN: They were traitors — honourable men!

44. *dear abide it* – pay dearly for it

61. *closet* – private chamber

62. *commons* – common people

69. *meet* – appropriate, fitting

ALL: The will! The testament! 80
SECOND CITIZEN: They were villains, murderers! The will!
Read the will.
ANTONY: You will compel me, then, to read the will?
Then make a ring about the corpse of Caesar
And let me show you him that made the will. 85
Shall I descend and will you give me leave?
SEVERAL CITIZENS: Come down.
SECOND CITIZEN: Descend.

Antony comes down.

FOURTH CITIZEN: A ring! Stand round.
FIRST CITIZEN: Stand from the hearse, stand from the body. 90
SECOND CITIZEN: Room for Antony, most noble Antony.
ANTONY: Nay, press not so upon me. Stand far off.
SEVERAL CITIZENS: Stand back! Room! Bear back.
ANTONY: If you have tears, prepare to shed them now.
You all do know this mantle. I remember 95
The first time ever Caesar put it on ...
Look, in this place ran Cassius' dagger through.
See what a rent the envious Casca made.
Through this the well-beloved Brutus stabbed
And as he plucked his cursed steel away, 100
Mark how the blood of Caesar followed it,
As rushing out of doors, ...
This was the most unkindest cut of all,
For when the noble Caesar saw him stab,
Ingratitude, more strong than traitors' arms, 105
Quite vanquished him. Then burst his mighty heart ...
O, what a fall was there, my countrymen! ...
FIRST CITIZEN: O piteous spectacle!
SECOND CITIZEN: O noble Caesar!
THIRD CITIZEN: O woeful day! 110
FOURTH CITIZEN: O traitors, villains!
FIRST CITIZEN: O most bloody sight!
SECOND CITIZEN: We will be revenged.
ALL: Revenge! About! Seek! Burn! Fire! Kill! Slay!
Let not a traitor live! 115
ANTONY: Stay, countrymen.
FIRST CITIZEN: Peace there! Hear the noble Antony.
SECOND CITIZEN: We'll hear him, we'll follow him,
we'll die with him.

90. *hearse* – funeral bier

95. *mantle* – cloak

98. *envious* – malicious; jealous

103. Antony says that Brutus' cut was the *most unkindest cut of all.* Perhaps this is because it was believed that Brutus was Caesar's illegitimate son. Caesar spared Brutus' life on more than one occasion and this fuelled the speculation of Caesar's paternity.

ANTONY: Good friends, sweet friends, let me not stir you up 120
To such a sudden flood of mutiny.
They that have done this deed are honourable ...
I come not, friends, to steal away your hearts.
I am no orator, as Brutus is.
But, as you know me all, a plain blunt man, 125
That love my friend ...
For I have neither wit, nor words, nor worth,
Action, nor utterance, nor the power of speech,
To stir men's blood. I only speak right on.
I tell you that which you yourselves do know. 130
Show you sweet Caesar's wounds, poor poor dumb mouths,
And bid them speak for me. But were I Brutus,
And Brutus Antony, there were an Antony
Would ruffle up your spirits and put a tongue
In every wound of Caesar that should move 135
The stones of Rome to rise and mutiny.
ALL: We'll mutiny.
FIRST CITIZEN: We'll burn the house of Brutus.
THIRD CITIZEN: Away, then! Come, seek the conspirators.
ANTONY: Yet hear me, countrymen! Yet hear me speak. 140
ALL: Peace, ho! Hear Antony. Most noble Antony!
ANTONY: Why, friends, you go to do you know not what.
Wherein hath Caesar thus deserved your loves?
Alas, you know not. I must tell you then.
You have forgot the will I told you of. 145
ALL: Most true. The will! Let's stay and hear the will.
ANTONY: Here is the will, and under Caesar's seal.
To every Roman citizen he gives,
To every several man, seventy-five drachmas.
SECOND CITIZEN: Most noble Caesar! 150
We'll revenge his death.
THIRD CITIZEN: O royal Caesar!
ANTONY: Hear me with patience.
ALL: Peace, ho!
ANTONY: Moreover, he hath left you all his walks, 155
His private arbours and new-planted orchards,
On this side Tiber. He hath left them you,
And to your heirs for ever, common pleasures,
To walk abroad, and recreate yourselves.
Here was a Caesar! When comes such another? 160
FIRST CITIZEN: Never, never. Come, away, away!
We'll burn his body in the holy place,
And with the brands fire the traitors' houses.
Take up the body.

124. *orator* – public speaker

127 – 129. Antony is being modest for rhetorical purposes.

149. *seventy-five drachmas* – in today's currency, about $50.

157. *Tiber* – The Tiber River, which supplied water, food, and transportation in Rome.

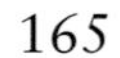

SECOND CITIZEN: Go fetch fire. 165
THIRD CITIZEN: Pluck down benches.
FOURTH CITIZEN: Pluck down forms, windows, any thing.

Exeunt Citizens with the body.

ANTONY: Now let it work. Mischief, thou art afoot,
Take thou what course thou wilt!

It is never good to bring bad news

(Antony and Cleopatra – Act 2, Scene 5)

To make peace with Octavius Caesar and to rescue Rome from outside attack, Antony has had to leave his beloved Cleopatra and return to Italy. To cement the newly made peace with Caesar and to assure everyone that he is still loyal to Rome, Antony has even agreed to marry Caesar's sister, Octavia. Meanwhile, back in Egypt, Cleopatra anxiously awaits any news from Rome about her only love, Antony. A Messenger finally arrives and is admitted into Cleopatra's presence.

CLEOPATRA: *[Excitedly.]* O, from Italy!
Ram thou thy fruitful tidings in mine ears,
That long time have been barren.
MESSENGER: *[Sadly and nervously.]* Madam, madam,—
CLEOPATRA: Antonius dead! — If thou say so, villain, 5
Thou killest thy mistress, but well and free,
If thou so yield him, there is gold, and here
My bluest veins to kiss, a hand that kings
Have lipped, and trembled kissing.
MESSENGER: First, madam, he is well. 10
CLEOPATRA: Why, there's more gold.
But, sirrah, mark, we use
To say the dead are well. Bring it to that,
The gold I give thee will I melt and pour
Down thy ill-uttering throat. 15
MESSENGER: Good madam, hear me.
CLEOPATRA: Well, go to, I will.
But there's no goodness in thy face. If Antony
Be free and healthful, so tart a favour
To trumpet such good tidings! If not well, 20
Thou shouldst come like a Fury crowned with snakes,
Not like a formal man.
MESSENGER: Will it please you hear me?
CLEOPATRA: I have a mind to strike thee ere thou speakest.
Yet if thou say Antony lives, is well, 25
Or friends with Caesar, or not captive to him,
I'll set thee in a shower of gold, and hail
Rich pearls upon thee.
MESSENGER: Madam, he's well.

2. *fruitful tidings* – good news

7. *yield* – report

8. *bluest veins* – It was believed that royalty had blue blood

21. *Fury* – According to Greek mythology, Furies were supernatural creatures that looked like winged women whose hair was made of snakes and whose eyes dripped blood. It was their function to punish criminals.

24. *ere* – before

36. *allay* – annul, set aside

40. *pack of matter* – the entire story

44. *bound* – joined in marriage

47. *Charmian* – one of Cleopatra's servants

53. *spurn* – kick

62. *boot thee* – reward you

CLEOPATRA: Well said. 30
MESSENGER: And friends with Caesar.
CLEOPATRA: Thou art an honest man.
MESSENGER: Caesar and he are greater friends than ever.
CLEOPATRA: Make thee a fortune from me.
MESSENGER: But yet, madam,— 35
CLEOPATRA: I do not like 'But yet,' it does allay
The good precedence. Fie upon 'But yet'!
'But yet' is as a gaoler to bring forth
Some monstrous malefactor. Prithee, friend,
Pour out the pack of matter to mine ear, 40
The good and bad together: he's friends with Caesar,
In state of health, thou sayest, and thou sayest, free.
MESSENGER: Free, madam! No, I made no such report.
He's bound unto Octavia.
CLEOPATRA: For what good turn? 45
MESSENGER: For the best turn in the bed.
CLEOPATRA: I am pale, Charmian.
MESSENGER: Madam, he's married to Octavia.
CLEOPATRA: The most infectious pestilence upon thee!

She strikes him down with repeated blows.

MESSENGER: Good madam, patience. 50
CLEOPATRA: What say you?

She strikes him again.

Hence,
Horrible villain, or I'll spurn thine eyes
Like balls before me! I'll unhair thy head!

She hales him up and down.

Thou shalt be whipped with wire, and stewed in brine, 55
Smarting in lingering pickle.
MESSENGER: Gracious madam,
I that do bring the news made not the match.
CLEOPATRA: Say 'tis not so, a province I will give thee,
And make thy fortunes proud. The blow thou hadst 60
Shall make thy peace for moving me to rage,
And I will boot thee with what gift beside
Thy modesty can beg.
MESSENGER: He's married, madam.

CLEOPATRA: Rogue, thou hast lived too long. 65

She draws a knife and threatens toward him.

MESSENGER: Nay, then I'll run.
What mean you, madam? I have made no fault.

He runs away into another room.

CHARMIAN: Good madam, keep yourself within yourself.
The man is innocent.
CLEOPATRA: Some innocents escape not the thunderbolt. 70
Melt Egypt into Nile and kindly creatures
Turn all to serpents! Call the slave again.
Though I am mad, I will not bite him. Call.
CHARMIAN: He is afeard to come.
CLEOPATRA: I will not hurt him. 75

Charmian exits.

These hands do lack nobility, that they strike
A meaner than myself ...

Re-enter Charmian and Messenger.

Come hither, sir.
Though it be honest, it is never good
To bring bad news. Give to a gracious message 80
An host of tongues, but let ill tidings tell
Themselves when they be felt.
MESSENGER: I have done my duty.
CLEOPATRA: Is he married?
I cannot hate thee worser than I do, 85
If thou again say 'Yes.'
MESSENGER: He's married, madam.
CLEOPATRA: The gods confound thee!
Dost thou hold there still?
MESSENGER: Should I lie, madam? 90
CLEOPATRA: O, I would thou didst,
So half my Egypt were submerged and made
A cistern for scaled snakes! Go, get thee hence.
Hadst thou Narcissus in thy face, to me
Thou wouldst appear most ugly. He is married? 95
MESSENGER: I crave your highness' pardon.

81. *host of tongues* – lengthy report

88. *confound* – destroy, confuse

93. *cistern* – container or pond
94. *Narcissus* – in Greek myth, he was so beautiful that he fell in love with his own reflection.

CLEOPATRA: He is married?
MESSENGER: Take no offence that I would not offend you:
To punish me for what you make me do.
Seems much unequal. He's married to Octavia. 100
CLEOPATRA: O, that his fault should make a knave of thee ...
Get thee hence.
The merchandise which thou hast brought from Rome
Are all too dear for me ...

104. *dear* – costly; grievous

Exit Messenger.

CHARMIAN: Good your highness, patience ... 105
CLEOPATRA: Lead me from hence. I faint,
O Iras, Charmian! 'Tis no matter.
Go to the fellow, good Alexas. Bid him
Report the feature of Octavia, her years,
Her inclination, let him not leave out 110
The colour of her hair. Bring me word quickly.

110. *inclination* – character; disposition

Exit Alexas.

Let him for ever go, let him not—Charmian,
Though he be painted one way like a Gorgon,
The other way's a Mars.
[To Mardian.*]* Bid you Alexas 115
Bring me word how tall she is. Pity me, Charmian,
But do not speak to me. Lead me to my chamber.

Exeunt.

113. *Gorgon* – monster so hideous that anyone who looks at it turns to stone.
114. *Mars* – Greek god of war

Gorgon

Pyramus and Thisbe

(A Midsummer Night's Dream –
Act 5, Scene 1)

We often think of the Elizabethan period as being the golden age of drama in England. Many great plays were written during this time — but unfortunately many terrible plays were also written. Shakespeare, as is evident in this selection, loved to poke fun at himself and his fellow playwrights. What follows is a tragedy that never fails to evoke tears — of laughter in the audience.

PROLOGUE: If we offend, it is with our good will.
That you should think, we come not to offend,
But with good will. To show our simple skill,
That is the true beginning of our end.
Consider then we come but in despite. 5
We do not come as minding to contest you,
Our true intent is. All for your delight
We are not here. That you should here repent you,
The actors are at hand and by their show
You shall know all that you are like to know, 10

Enter Pyramus and Thisbe, Wall, Moonshine, and Lion.

Gentles, perchance you wonder at this show,
But wonder on, till truth make all things plain.
This man is Pyramus, if you would know;
This beauteous lady Thisby is certain.
This man, with lime and rough-cast, doth present 15
Wall, that vile Wall which did these lovers sunder.
And through Wall's chink, poor souls, they are content
To whisper. At the which let no man wonder.
This man, with lanthorn, dog, and bush of thorn,
Presenteth Moonshine. For, if you will know, 20
By moonshine did these lovers think no scorn
To meet at Ninus' tomb, there, there to woo.
This grisly beast, which Lion hight by name,
The trusty Thisby, coming first by night,
Did scare away, or rather did affright. 25
And, as she fled, her mantle she did fall,
Which Lion vile with bloody mouth did stain.
Anon comes Pyramus, sweet youth and tall,
And finds his trusty Thisby's mantle slain.
Whereat, with blade, with bloody blameful blade, 30

When reading this speech, pay careful attention to the punctuation. The speaker of the Prologue gets it all wrong and the result is nonsense. The comma at the end of line 10 is also intentional. It implies that the Prologue has built to a point and then lost his train of thought.

All the actors in this performance are amateur. In playing this brief, tedious scene, they are so bad that they are good. They are entertaining in their ineptness.

17. *chink* – hole (in a wall)

19. *lanthorn* – lantern

21. *think no scorn* – were not too proud

23. *hight* – is called

26. *mantle* – cloak

28. *Anon* – straight away

30 – 31. The excessive use of alliteration was Shakespeare's attempt to parody other dramatists' abuse of the device.

31. *broached* – pierced
32. *tarrying* – waiting
34. *twain* – both
35. *At large discourse* – talk about at length

The actor playing Pyramus is characterized by his tendency to over-act everything. He exaggerates his voice and his gestures. Once again Shakespeare is poking fun at his colleagues and competitors.

51. *eyne* – eye
52. *Jove* – king of the gods

He bravely broached his boiling bloody breast.
And Thisby, tarrying in mulberry shade,
His dagger drew, and died. For all the rest,
Let Lion, Moonshine, Wall, and lovers twain
At large discourse, while here they do remain. 35

Exeunt Prologue, Thisbe, Lion, and Moonshine.

WALL: In this same interlude it doth befall
That I, one Snout by name, present a wall.
And such a wall, as I would have you think,
That had in it a crannied hole or chink,
Through which the lovers, Pyramus and Thisby, 40
Did whisper often very secretly.
This loam, this rough-cast and this stone doth show
That I am that same wall, the truth is so.
And this the cranny is, right and sinister,
Through which the fearful lovers are to whisper.

Enter Pyramus.

PYRAMUS: O grim-looked night! O night with hue so black!
O night, which ever art when day is not! 45
O night, O night! Alack, alack, alack,
I fear my Thisby's promise is forgot!
And thou, O wall, O sweet, O lovely wall,
That standest between her father's ground and mine!
Thou wall, O wall, O sweet and lovely wall, 50
Show me thy chink, to blink through with mine eyne!

Wall holds up his fingers through which Pyramus looks through.

Thanks, courteous wall. Jove shield thee well for this!
But what see I? No Thisby do I see.
O wicked wall, through whom I see no bliss!
Cursed be thy stones for thus deceiving me! 55

Enter Thisbe.

THISBE: O wall, full often hast thou heard my moans,
For parting my fair Pyramus and me!
My cherry lips have often kissed thy stones, 60
Thy stones with lime and hair knit up in thee.

Pyramus: I see a voice. Now will I to the chink,
To spy an I can hear my Thisby's face.
Thisby!
Thisbe: My love thou art, my love I think. 65
Pyramus: Think what thou wilt, I am thy lover's grace ...
O kiss me through the hole of this vile wall!
Thisbe: I kiss the wall's hole, not your lips at all.
Pyramus: Wilt thou at Ninny's tomb meet me straightway?
Thisbe: 'Tide life, 'tide death, I come without delay. 70

Exeunt Pyramus and Thisbe.

Wall: Thus have I, Wall, my part discharged so
And, being done, thus Wall away doth go.

Wall exits. Enter Lion and Moonshine.

Lion: You, ladies, you, whose gentle hearts do fear
The smallest monstrous mouse that creeps on floor,
May now perchance both quake and tremble here, 75
When lion rough in wildest rage doth roar.
Then know that I, one Snug the joiner, am
A lion-fell, nor else no lion's dam.
For, if I should as lion come in strife
Into this place, 'twere pity on my life. 80
Moonshine: This lanthorn doth the horned moon present.
Myself the man in the moon do seem to be.
All that I have to say, is, to tell you that the
lanthorn is the moon. I, the man in the moon, this
thorn-bush, my thorn-bush, and this dog, my dog. 85

Enter Thisbe.

Thisbe: This is old Ninny's tomb. Where is my love?
Lion: *(Roaring)* Oh——

Thisbe drops her mantle and runs off.
Lion shakes Thisbe's mantle in his mouth, and exits.
Enter Pyramus.

Pyramus: Sweet Moon, I thank thee for thy sunny beams.
I thank thee, Moon, for shining now so bright,
For, by thy gracious, golden, glittering gleams, 90
I trust to take of truest Thisby sight.
But stay, O spite!

62 – 63. Notice how the actor playing Pyramus mixes up the senses. He sees a voice and he goes to hear a face.

63. *an* – if

70. *'tide* – come

78. *lion-fell* – cruel lion

100. *fell* – cruel
101. *Fates* – In Greek mythology, the three Fates were sisters who spun out the thread of life and who determined when one's life would end by cutting the thread.
104. *wherefore* – why

109. *confound* – confuse, destroy
111. *pap* – breast

But mark, poor knight,
What dreadful dole is here!
Eyes, do you see? 95
How can it be?
O dainty duck! O dear!
Thy mantle good,
What, stained with blood!
Approach, ye Furies fell! 100
O Fates, come, come,
Cut thread and thrum,
Quail, crush, conclude, and quell!

PYRAMUS: O wherefore, Nature, didst thou lions frame?
Since lion vile hath here deflowered my dear — 105
Which is—no, no—which was the fairest dame
That lived, that loved, that liked, that looked with cheer.
Come, tears, confound,
Out, sword, and wound 110
The pap of Pyramus.
Ay, that left pap,
Where heart doth hop.

Stabs himself.

Thus die I, thus, thus, thus.
Now am I dead, 115
Now am I fled.
My soul is in the sky.
Tongue, lose thy light;
Moon take thy flight.

Exit Moonshine.

Now die, die, die, die, die. 120

Dies. Re-enter Thisbe.

THISBE: Asleep, my love?
What, dead, my dove?
O Pyramus, arise!
Speak, speak. Quite dumb?
Dead, dead? A tomb 125
Must cover thy sweet eyes.
These My lips,
This cherry nose,

These yellow cowslip cheeks,
Are gone, are gone. 130
Lovers, make moan.
His eyes were green as leeks.
O Sisters Three,
Come, come to me,
With hands as pale as milk. 135
Lay them in gore,
Since you have shore
With shears his thread of silk.
Tongue, not a word.
Come, trusty sword. 140
Come, blade, my breast imbrue.

Stabs herself.

And, farewell, friends,
Thus Thisby ends.
Adieu, adieu, adieu.

Dies.

133. *Sisters Three* – the three Fates. See note for line 101.

137. *shore* – shorn, cut

141. *imbrue* – make bloody

End of the Unit Activities:

- In groups of two to six, choose a scene to prepare for the class. Some doubling of parts may be necessary. You may choose to use props and costumes as part of your presentation.

- As a variation of the above assignment, do a gender reversal in casting your scene. In other words, have the boys play the female roles and vice versa. What effect is thereby created?

- In groups, rewrite the scene into everyday speech with a modern day context. Be prepared to present your play to the class.

- Prepare a video of a scene. If you prefer, rather than memorize your parts, you can improvise the basic situation and dialogue.

- Create a story board or comic book version of any scene.

- Organize a Shakespeare Festival. Invite other classes to be the audience for your group presentations. Use the school theatre if you have one. Videotape the performances.

Reprinted with special permission of King Features Syndicate.

Sonnets

Act Three:

Not marble, nor the gilded monuments shall outlive these Sonnets

If Shakespeare had not written a single play, he would still be remembered today for his exquisite sonnets. Shakespeare did not invent the sonnet form. Petrarch (1304 – 1374) has that distinction. Sir Thomas Wyatt and others developed an English variation of the Petrarchan sonnet. However, Shakespeare so excelled in the form that today the English sonnet is better known as the Shakespearean sonnet.

The sonnet contains a very formalized structure. It consists of fourteen lines made up of three quatrains and a climactic rhyming couplet. Most sonnets utilize the following rhyme scheme:

abab cdcd efef gg.

The sonnet form is ideal for expressing powerful emotions on such serious subjects as love, death, permanence of literature, and reverence for God. Usually, the three quatrains contain different examples of, or comments on, a theme or powerful emotion. The last two lines serve as a climactic conclusion to the piece.

Besides his collection of 154 sonnets, Shakespeare also included a number of sonnets within his plays. The following is from *Romeo and Juliet:*

Two households, both alike in dignity,
In fair Verona, where we lay our scene,
From ancient grudge break to new mutiny,
Where civil blood makes civil hands unclean.
From forth the fatal loins of these two foes 5
A pair of star-crossed lovers take their life,
Whose misadventured piteous overthrows
Doth with their death bury their parents' strife.
The fearful passage of their death-marked love,
And the continuance of their parents' rage, 10
Which, but their children's end, naught could remove,
Is now the two hours' traffic of our stage.
The which if you with patient ears attend,
What here shall miss, our toil shall strive to mend.

3. *mutiny* – violence

6. *star-crossed* – ill-fated. The Elizabethans believed that destiny and character were, to a degree, determined by the stars.

7. *overthrows* – downfalls; death

11. *naught* – nothing

12. *two hours' traffic* – Perhaps a clue that when plays were performed at the Globe, they were edited to fit into a two-hour performance. *Romeo and Juliet*, if acted in its entirety, would take just under four hours.

Shall I compare thee to a summer's day?

Shall I compare thee to a summer's day?
Thou art more lovely and more temperate.
Rough winds do shake the darling buds of May,
And summer's lease hath all too short a date.
Sometime too hot the eye of heaven shines, 5
And often is his gold complexion dimmed,
And every fair from fair sometime declines,
By chance or nature's changing course untrimmed.
But thy eternal summer shall not fade
Nor lose possession of that fair thou owest, 10
Nor shall Death brag thou wanderest in his shade,
When in eternal lines to time thou growest.
  So long as men can breathe or eyes can see,
  So long lives this and this gives life to thee.

4. *lease* – term
date – duration
5. *eye of heaven* – the sun

7. "And every attractive person eventually declines in beauty"
8. *untrimmed* – made less beautiful
10. *owest* – possess
12. Immortalized in lines of poetry, the subject will live forever.
14. *this* – i.e. this sonnet

Devouring Time, blunt thou the lion's paws

Devouring Time, blunt thou the lion's paws,
And make the earth devour her own sweet brood.
Pluck the keen teeth from the fierce tiger's jaws,
And burn the long-lived phoenix in her blood.
Make glad and sorry seasons as thou fleet'st, 5
And do whatever thou wilt, swift-footed Time,
To the wide world and all her fading sweets.
But I forbid thee one most heinous crime:
O, carve not with thy hours my love's fair brow,
Nor draw no lines there with thine antique pen. 10
Him in thy course untainted do allow
For beauty's pattern to succeeding men.
Yet, do thy worst, old Time. Despite thy wrong,
My love shall in my verse ever live young.

4. *phoenix* – legendary bird who consumed itself in its own fire and from that fire, was reborn.
5. *fleet'st* – pass swiftly
8. *heinous* – shockingly evil
10. *antique* – aging
11. *untainted* – unblemished

phoenix

When to the sessions of sweet silent thought

1. *sessions* – court hearings

2. *Remembrance of Things Past* became the title for French writer Marcel Proust's well-known seven part novel, written between 1913 and 1927.

4. *new wail* – mourn anew ... *dear time's waste* – the loss of my precious youth

6. *dateless* – endless

8. *expense* – loss

9. *grievances forgone* – old subjects that caused grief

10. *heavily* – mournfully

tell – count

When to the sessions of sweet silent thought
I summon up remembrance of things past,
I sigh the lack of many a thing I sought,
And with old woes new wail my dear time's waste.
Then can I drown an eye, unused to flow, 5
For precious friends hid in death's dateless night,
And weep afresh love's long since cancelled woe,
And moan the expense of many a vanished sight.
Then can I grieve at grievances foregone,
And heavily from woe to woe tell over 10
The sad account of fore-bemoaned moan,
Which I new pay as if not paid before.
But if the while I think on thee, dear friend,
All losses are restored and sorrows end.

No longer mourn for me when I am dead

No longer mourn for me when I am dead
Than you shall hear the surly sullen bell
Give warning to the world that I am fled
From this vile world, with vilest worms to dwell.
Nay, if you read this line, remember not 5
The hand that writ it, for I love you so
That I in your sweet thoughts would be forgot
If thinking on me then should make you woe.
Oh, if, I say, you look upon this verse
When I perhaps compounded am with clay, 10
Do not so much as my poor name rehearse.
But let your love even with my life decay,
  Lest the wise world should look into your moan
  And mock you with me after I am gone.

1. *No longer mourn* – i.e. Mourn no longer
2. *surly* – gloomy
11. *rehearse* – repeat
13. *lest* – for fear that

Let me not to the marriage of true minds

2. *impediments* – In marriage ceremonies, the congregation is asked if they "know of any just impediment why these persons should not be joined together."
5. *ever-fixed mark* – constant guide
6. *tempest* – storm
7. *bark* – small boat
8. *height* – altitude. One can navigate by taking measurements of certain stars.
9. *Time's fool* – one who is mocked by time
10. *compass* – reach
12. *doom* – Doomsday, the end of time

Some read the climactic concluding couplet as suggesting that the author is proud of his contribution to the world of writing.

Let me not to the marriage of true minds
Admit impediments. Love is not love
Which alters when it alteration finds,
Or bends with the remover to remove.
O no! It is an ever-fixed mark 5
That looks on tempests and is never shaken.
It is the star to every wandering bark,
Whose worth's unknown, although his height be taken.
Love's not Time's fool, though rosy lips and cheeks
Within his bending sickle's compass come. 10
Love alters not with his brief hours and weeks,
But bears it out even to the edge of doom.
  If this be error and upon me proved,
  I never writ, nor no man ever loved.

My mistress' eyes are nothing like the sun

My mistress' eyes are nothing like the sun.
Coral is far more red than her lips' red.
If snow be white, why then her breasts are dun;
If hairs be wires, black wires grow on her head.
I have seen roses damasked, red and white, 5
But no such roses see I in her cheeks.
And in some perfumes is there more delight
Than in the breath that from my mistress reeks.
I love to hear her speak, yet well I know
That music hath a far more pleasing sound. 10
I grant I never saw a goddess go.
My mistress, when she walks, treads on the ground.
And yet, by heaven, I think my love as rare
As any she belied with false compare.

This sonnet strikes at the sentimentality expressed by other sonnet writers. Here Shakespeare goes out of his way to deny his love any of the qualities so praised in other sonnets.

3. *dun* – dull brown
5. *damasked* – pink and white variegated
8. *reeks* – breathes
11. *go* – walk
14. "As any woman misrepresented through false comparisons."

End of the Unit Activities:

- Write a journal response to any two sonnets.
- Rewrite any sonnet in the form of a personal letter. Do not hesitate to add specific details to make your letter sound more realistic.
- Create a poster or collage in which you illustrate one of the sonnets. You may choose to use magazine illustrations and/or original art work to complete your poster or collage.
- Rewrite any sonnet into everyday speech. Try to retain the rhyming scheme if you can.
- Write your own sonnet on any subject you wish. Accompany your sonnet with an appropriate graphic.
- Write a parody of any of the sonnets in this unit. Use as many of the original words as you deem appropriate.

Epilogue

Epilogue:

Our revels now are ended

In the play, *The Tempest,* the magician and play-maker Prospero speaks for Shakespeare as he dismisses his actors from the scene:

> Our revels now are ended. These our actors,
> As I foretold you, were all spirits and
> Are melted into air, into thin air,
> And, like the baseless fabric of this vision,
> The cloud-capped towers, the gorgeous palaces, 5
> The solemn temples, the great globe itself,
> Yea, all which it inherit, shall dissolve
> And, like this insubstantial pageant faded,
> Leave not a rack behind. We are such stuff
> As dreams are made on, and our little life 10
> Is rounded with a sleep.
> (*The Tempest* – Act 4, Scene 1)

9. *rack* – cloud or mist

There is no more fitting quotation to end this introduction to Shakespeare's works. It is hoped that you have enjoyed the revels and that you have been enriched by the experience.

However, even Prospero recognizes that there comes a time for actors to take off their make-up and costumes, to put aside the roles they have been playing and to re-enter the real world. In a way, we readers are like actors in that, for a short time, through the magic of poetry and imagination, we inhabit a fantastical world of unforgettable characters, cloud-capped towers, gorgeous palaces and solemn temples.

The value of any exposure to Shakespeare lies in the fact that when we re-enter the real world, we are the richer for having had that experience. We grow by it and are forever touched by the influence of his characters and his words.

Shakespeare is indeed "Not of an age but for all time" and for all people.

REVIEWERS

The publishers and editors would like to thank the following educators for contributing their valuable expertise during the development of the *Global Shakespeare Series*:

Nancy Alford
Sir John A. Macdonald High School
Hubley, Nova Scotia

Dr. Philip Allingham
Golden Secondary School
Golden, British Columbia

Peter Atkinson
St. Matthew High School
Orléans, Ontario

Sandie Bender
Carleton Roman Catholic School Board
Nepean, Ontario

Carol Brown
Walter Murray Collegiate Institute
Saskatoon, Saskatchewan

Rod Brown
Wellington Secondary School
Nanaimo, British Columbia

Brian Dietrich
Queen Elizabeth Senior Secondary School
Surrey, British Columbia

Alison Douglas
McNally High School
Edmonton, Alberta

Kim Driscoll
Adam Scott Secondary School
Peterborough, Ontario

Burton Eikleberry
Grants Pass High School
Grants Pass, Oregon

Gloria Evans
Lakewood Junior Secondary School
Prince George, British Columbia

Professor Averil Gardner
Memorial University
St. John's, Newfoundland

Joyce L. Halsey
Lee's Summit North High School
Lee's Summit, Missouri

Carol Innazzo
St. Bernard's College
West Essendon, Victoria, Australia

Winston Jackson
Belmont Secondary School
Victoria, British Columbia

Marion Jenkins
Glenlyon-Norfolk School
Victoria, British Columbia

Dr. Sharon Johnston
Maynard Evans High School
Orlando, Florida

Jean Jonkers
William J. Dean Technical High School
Holyoke, Massachusetts

Beverly Joyce
Brockton High School
Brockton, Massachusetts

Judy Kayse
Huntsville High School
Huntsville, Texas

Doreen Kennedy
Vancouver Technical Secondary School
Burnaby, British Columbia

Ross Laing
Sir Wilfrid Laurier Secondary School
Orléans, Ontario

Gerard Lavelle
Lester B. Pearson High School
Gloucester, Ontario

Ed Metcalfe
Fleetwood Park Secondary School
Surrey, British Columbia

Janine Modestow
William J. Dean Technical High School
Holyoke, Massachusetts

Steve Naylor
Salmon Arm Senior Secondary School
Salmon Arm, British Columbia

Kathleen Oakes
Implay City Senior High School
Romeo, Michigan

Carla O'Brien
Lakewood Junior Secondary School
Prince George, British Columbia

Bruce L. Pagni
Waukegan High School
Waukegan, Illinois

Larry Peters
Lisgar Collegiate
Ottawa, Ontario

Margaret Poetschke
Lisgar Collegiate
Ottawa, Ontario

Jeff Purse
Walter Murray Collegiate Institute
Saskatoon, Saskatchewan

Phyllis B. Schwartz
Lord Byng Secondary School
Vancouver, BC

Grant Shaw
Elmwood High School
Winnipeg, Manitoba

Jim Sherman
South Carleton District High School
Richmond, Ontario

Debarah Shoultz
Columbus North High School
Columbus, Indiana

Tim Turner
Kiona-Benton High School
Benton City, Washington

James Walsh
Vernon Township High School
Vernon, New Jersey

Ted Wholey
Sir John A. Macdonald High School
Hubley, Nova Scotia

Beverly Winny
Adam Scott Secondary School
Peterborough, Ontario

About the Series Editors

Dom Saliani, Senior Editor of the *Global Shakespeare Series*, is the Curriculum Leader of English at Sir Winston Churchill High School in Calgary, Alberta. He has been an English teacher for over 25 years and has published a number of poetry and literature anthologies.

Chris Ferguson is the Curriculum Director for the Central Texas Tech Prep Consortium in Temple, Texas. Formerly the Department Head of English at Burnet High School in Burnet, Texas, she has taught English, drama, and speech communications for over 15 years.

Dr. Tim Scott is an English teacher at Melbourne Grammar School in Victoria, Australia, where he directs a Shakespeare production every year. He wrote his Ph.D. thesis on Elizabethan drama.

ACKNOWLEDGEMENTS

IGNITION Design and Communications: 23, 31, 32, 35, 36, 37, 38, 60, 65, 68, 76, 87, 93; pantaloon from engraving by Claude Gillot (1673-1722): 23; bear-baiting from Charles Knight's *Pictorial Edition of the Works of Shakspere, 1839-1843*: 31; Ophelia by J. Millais from The Tate Gallery: 27; vintner's bush from a medieval manuscript: 38; Romulus and Remus engraving from a Roman medal in G. du Choul's *Discours de la Religion des Anciens Romains*, 1567: 68; Paul Morin: 72; phoenix from Geffrey Whitney, *A Choice of Emblems*, (1586): 87; Nicholas Vitacco: 7, 21, 41, 83, 93.